D1495598

BECKHAM

AND

FERGUSON

DIVIDED THEY STAND

BECKHAM

AND

FERGUSON

DIVIDED THEY STAND

JASON TOMAS

SUTTON PUBLISHING

First published in 2003 by
Sutton Publishing Limited · Phoenix Mill
Thrupp · Stroud · Gloucestershire · GL5 2BU

Copyright © Jason Tomas, 2003

All rights reserved. No part of this publication may be reproduced, stored in a retrieval system, or transmitted, in any form, or by any means, electronic, mechanical, photocopying, recording or otherwise, without the prior permission of the publisher and copyright holder.

Jason Tomas hereby asserts the moral right to be identified as the author of this work.

British Library Cataloguing in Publication Data
A catalogue record for this book is available from the British Library.

ISBN 0-7509-3675-4

Typeset in 12/18.5 pt Sabon.
Typesetting and origination by
Sutton Publishing Limited.
Printed and bound in England by
J.H. Haynes & Co. Ltd, Sparkford.

Contents

Introduction

When Sir Alex Ferguson got off the plane with the Manchester United squad on a trip to Malaysia, he was rather taken aback by a member of the official greeting party's reference to him as 'Your Excellency'.

But the description is not inappropriate in the context of Fergie's stature as a football manager, and the amazing effect that football can have on people's lives. Television has helped make the game more popular than ever. It reaches every level of society throughout the world. Hence the fact that when Fergie crossed swords with David Beckham, the most famous player in the world, it was never going to be a matter of merely passing interest.

It is difficult to think of any relationship in sport that has attracted as much attention as that between Fergie and Beckham. Their areas of conflict became such big talking points among the general public that the pair became sport's equivalent of Elizabeth Taylor and Richard Burton or Nicole Kidman and Tom Cruise. The one aspect of their relationship that is beyond any doubt is that the storyline – brought into millions of homes through the media – has been as compelling as that of any television soap opera.

Ferguson has never come across another player like David Beckham during a glittering 17-year United career in which he has steered this biggest and most glamorous of clubs to 15 honours, including an historic European Champions League, Championship and FA Cup treble and two Championship–FA Cup doubles. Of the 915 first-team matches United had played under his management up to the start of the 2003/04 season, only 177 were lost.

During this period Ferguson rubbed shoulders with many top-class performers and, despite the increase in the power wielded by such players, his sense of authority was not seriously challenged by any of them. But Beckham, a young man who has become much, much more than a star footballer, and whose status as a cultural icon is further enhanced by the professional nationwide respect for his inspiring performances as England captain, is the one who has come closest to it.

The intriguing story of the link between the 61-year-old Ferguson and the 28-year-old Beckham is one of two totally different personalities, with totally different attitudes and mentalities.

A key factor that brought them together, in addition to Beckham's ability, was their commitment to Manchester United. Beckham was an avid United supporter as a boy and his career there was a dream come true. Ferguson, the hardest of taskmasters in teaching players sound professional habits and a manager with the courage to give inexperienced youngsters the chance to prove themselves at first-team level, played a major part in that.

But Beckham's life changed as a result of his ever-growing celebrity status and his marriage to

Posh Spice, and Ferguson found his position of authority in the relationship increasingly difficult to sustain.

The more success they achieved together, the more it seemed Old Trafford was unlikely to remain big enough to hold both of them. On top of this was Fergie's feeling that he needed to change various aspects of United's play to allow the club to make further progress, and that Beckham, having been an integral part of the team for eight years, had reached his sell-by date for that reason alone.

But even though they have now parted, the Fergie–Beckham soap opera has not ended. Instead, with both men striving to show that they can get on perfectly well without the other, it is destined to provide more must-see episodes.

Chapter One

A Clash of Opposites

Sir Alex Ferguson believes that the relationship between a manager and a player can never be totally harmonious. 'Even when there is mutual respect and liking, the relationship between a manager and player can be complex,' he said in his 1999 autobiography, *Managing my Life*. 'Success for the team is their shared objective but there is an obvious difference in the pressures and anxieties that they experience and that difference contains the seeds of conflict. Some of the best alliances between player and manager have been volatile.'

Being the aggressive, fiery person that he is, Ferguson has had countless personal experiences of this volatility throughout his career. In his Aberdeen days one of the players with whom he had the most ups and downs was Steve Archibald – interestingly, a man he regarded as a kindred spirit. The centre-forward, much admired by Fergie because of his hunger for success and single-mindedness, had no fears about questioning the manager's ideas and methods. As a result, he spent so much time in Ferguson's office arguing over various points that Fergie referred to the chair he used as 'The Archibald Chair'.

In its way, Fergie's relationship with Beckham was even more intriguing. The link between them did much to help Ferguson establish himself as the most successful manager in the history of English football, and to make Beckham its most famous and richest player.

Ferguson's Manchester United had achieved success before Beckham came into the first-team picture in the mid-1990s, but Beckham, a member of the new generation of young stars at Old Trafford, was to play a major part in that picture, becoming ever more dazzling. Beckham was a key member of the team who achieved the historic treble of the European Champions League, Championship and FA Cup in 1999. He was a member of four other Championship-winning sides, and another FA Cup-winning team. Only in two of his seven seasons of regular first-team action at United did they fail to get their hands on a trophy. His contribution to this run of glorious achievement was mirrored in a multitude of personal honours. In addition to his appointment as England captain and his OBE, he was twice runner-up in the FIFA World Footballer of the Year poll and was BBC TV Sports Personality of the Year in 2001.

His image as the perfect football role model, and the extent to which it has been reinforced by his looks and by the celebrity show-business lifestyle he entered into with his marriage to Victoria 'Posh Spice' Adams, meant Beckham's importance to United was no less pronounced off the field. As the ultimate sporting icon, he was looked upon as a key component in the club's burgeoning world-wide commercial empire. The view that the name Manchester United represents a brand that virtually amounts to a licence to print money through endorsements, advertising and sponsorship was particularly easy to appreciate during Beckham's career with the club. Referring to Manchester United's bid to exploit their popularity in Asia (where they have 16.6 million fans, compared with 11 million in the United Kingdom, and where Beckham's status is God-like), one expert said at the time of Beckham's transfer: 'From a marketing perspective, David Beckham is a snip at £25–30 million. He is worth that as a footballer, even in today's depressed market. As a brand in his own right, he is worth at least double. Any club that can help him develop his profile stand to make millions.'

But while Manchester United and Beckham seemed perfect for each other, there was another side to the story. Behind the scenes of the Old Trafford 'Theatre of Dreams', Beckham and Ferguson's relationship was conducted against a background of increasing tension. There had always been areas of conflict in their dealings with each other, comparatively minor irritations that are common in all manager–player relationships. But the longer they worked together, the more these sharply contrasting figures epitomising the old and new faces of British football appeared to need the game's equivalent of a marriage guidance counsellor. Opposites attract, but the differences that help bring them together, that enable them to complement each other, can just as easily push them apart. At the end, when Ferguson did what had once seemed unthinkable – show Beckham the Old Trafford exit – the pair appeared to be virtually incompatible.

The first recorded instance of Beckham and Ferguson not being in total harmony came in 1997. Beckham had met and fallen in love with Victoria Adams, and Fergie says he had to 'order' him to switch off his mobile phone because he was spending so much time in conversation with her before the European Champions League semi-final against Borussia Dortmund. The same year, with Victoria having moved temporarily to Ireland, Fergie has said that he told him he was making too many trips to see her instead of remaining in Manchester to concentrate on his training.

In July 1999, Beckham and Ferguson allegedly clashed over Fergie's refusal to allow the player an extra three days for his honeymoon. Two months later, it was reported that Beckham was hit with a fine as a result of a curfew-breaking appearance at a London Fashion Week party the night before United were due to fly out for the European Champions League match against Sturm Graz. Then, towards the end of 1999, Beckham – whose main family home was near London – is reported to have clashed with Fergie over the player's request to join the team at Heathrow for the World Club Championship trip to Tokyo. Fergie is said to have ordered him to start the journey with his colleagues in Manchester.

In February 2000, Beckham and Fergie were reported to have had another bust-up when the player went awol from a training session two days before a Premiership match against Leeds. Beckham's explanation was that his son Brooklyn had been taken ill and he had had to look after him because Victoria had gone out. Ferguson dropped him from the squad. Twelve months later came the mother of all Beckham–Fergie dust-ups – the infamous flying boot affair that was to prove the beginning of the end of their relationship.

Heated dressing-room rows are common in professional football, especially at half-time or immediately after matches when emotions are running particularly high. It has even been known for players to trade punches with each other, or with their manager or coach.

The atmosphere in the Manchester United dressing room after their 2–0 FA Cup defeat by Arsenal at Old Trafford on 15 February 2003 was certainly highly charged. The tension stemmed from Ferguson's disappointment in his team's performance and his belief that Beckham had contributed to the Gunners' second goal by not tracking his immediate opponent (left-back Ashley Cole) in the move that led to it. It was alleged that in the dressing room afterwards, Ferguson, already in one of his trademark high-octane moods as he criticised Beckham, exploded when the player (who had been substituted) voiced his disagreement.

Ferguson's reaction was to lash out at a stray boot, accidentally propelling it into the air and on to Beckham's face. It caused a cut above Beckham's left eye, for which he needed two stitches. According to one source quoted in the *Daily Mail*: 'All hell broke loose [when the boot hit Beckham]. When Beckham's wound started to bleed, the player shouted: "F***ing hell, my head is covered with blood." Ferguson shrugged and told the physio: "Just f***ing patch him up." It was amazing.' There was a rumour, vehemently denied by Beckham's management company, that Beckham spat at Ferguson, hitting him on his jacket.

Another report claimed that Victoria, having been dissuaded from confronting Ferguson personally over the incident, encouraged David to show the world what the manager had done to him. The following morning, when Beckham left his Cheshire home to go to the United training ground, he made no attempt to hide the medical tape on his wound. The newspaper photographers camped outside his home must have thought that Christmas had come early. For once, the woolly hat usually jammed down over his ears was missing and he was not wearing his sunglasses. Uncharacteristically, he even stopped his black Harley-Davidson jeep to allow the snappers to get better shots.

This was not a move guaranteed to take some of the heat out of his relationship with Fergie. Indeed, Beckham's reaction to the incident might help explain why Fergie steadfastly refused to make a public apology to the player. When questioned about the incident in an interview with Granada TV, he just said: 'That happens in a dressing room. It's a freak act of nature. It happens and it's over.' In other media interviews he described Beckham's injury as a 'graze', and joked that if he could hit balls as well as he hit the boot that struck Beckham, he would have kept on playing.

But Beckham, who allegedly told friends that his situation with Fergie was now untenable and that he was at the end of his tether, struggled to see the funny side. In the ensuing weeks, with the spotlight focusing ever more intently on their rift, Fergie was hardly a barrel of laughs on the subject either. Even talking about Beckham at press conferences seemed to touch a raw nerve in him. This was plain for all to see during the build-up to Beckham's transfer, when the manager was repeatedly put under pressure by the media to explain why he had been leaving the player out of United's starting line-up. The media had expressly been told not to mention the subject at the press conference for the match at Tottenham on 26 April. When one radio journalist did, Fergie exploded.

'Sir Alex,' the journalist said, 'I suppose you must be sick of all the hype surrounding David Beckham since Wednesday [on that day

Ferguson had named Beckham as a substitute for the second leg European Champions League quarter-final against Real Madrid, and Beckham had come on and scored two goals].' Ferguson, looking like a candidate for a heart attack, turned the air blue. The gist of his reaction was: 'You have been told not to f***ing ask that, right? Cut that off, cut that off [pointing to the journalist's tape-recorder]. F***ing idiots you all are. You do that again, and you won't be coming back here. You f***ing sell your newspapers and your radio shows on the back of this club.'

Even a few weeks after Beckham's transfer, when United were on tour in the United States, the B-word got to Fergie again. Before United's friendly clash with Celtic in Seattle, a journalist asked if he had any words for the people of the city who had been looking forward to seeing Beckham play. Ferguson fixed him with a hostile stare. 'No, no words at all.'

The relationship might have ended, but as Ferguson and Beckham strive to further their careers without each other, the speculation surrounding both sides in the story continues to rumble on and on.

Not everyone in the ranks of prominent present or past professional football figures considered that Beckham was essential to United. Some suggested that he had been at Old Trafford for too long and that both parties would benefit from a change. All clubs need to keep improving their teams and at clubs of Manchester United's stature, where the overall standard is so high and there is so much star spending money available, there are precious few players who cannot be deemed expendable.

There was a school of thought (albeit a small one) that Beckham was approaching the end of his United shelf-life in his accustomed role as a right-side midfielder; that he did not have the positional sense to compensate fully for his lack of pace against top-class opposition and was beginning to struggle to get on the ball in tight games. To an extent, in the 2002/03 season such views seemed to be supported by United's results and performances during the two periods when Ferguson left him out of the team. They did not win every match, but they hardly fell apart.

Beckham started in only two of their nine matches in December 2002. Of the other seven (which produced five victories and two defeats), he was not even in the squad for the big Premiership clashes against Arsenal and Liverpool, both of which United won. It was a similar story at the tail-end of the season, when Beckham was only partially involved, or not involved at all, in six of United's last 13 matches. The most important of these half-a-dozen games, which in total brought United two wins and two draws, was the one against Arsenal at Highbury. United's hugely impressive performance in getting a 2–2 draw – with Beckham on the bench but not used – was a big factor in their pipping the Gunners to the Championship. Another Premiership match in which he played no part in the action was the 6–2 thrashing of Newcastle at St James's Park, one of the most stunning results of the season.

And with Beckham deployed as a sub, Liverpool, who had beaten United 2–0 in the League Cup Final, went down 4–0.

The wounded pride that Beckham must have experienced during these periods was never more difficult to bear than when Ferguson announced his team for the Champions League second leg against Real on 23 April 2003. If ever there seemed to be a perfect challenge for a football icon, and especially one with David Beckham's attacking ability, it was the target of helping United cancel out Real's 3–1 first leg lead to register a momentous aggregate victory in front of their own fans. The decision to use him as a substitute seemed almost an insult, not least because the player who edged him out of the starting line-up – Juan Sebastian Veron – had been something of an Old Trafford under-achiever and was not fully match fit.

True, Real's left back Roberto Carlos was one of the opponents who had achieved the greatest degree of mastery over Beckham in the past. Beckham had certainly struggled to make any headway against him in the first leg. But the England captain has a habit of pulling something special out of the bag when it is most needed or if he feels he has a point to prove. Coming on after 63 minutes, Beckham left no room for doubt about this when he scored two of the goals that brought United a 4–3 win after they had been 1–0 and then 3–1 behind.

It might not have meant much in the context of Real's overall ascendancy and the aggregate result, but Beckham's performance raised the obvious question of what might have happened had he been in the team from the start. The tabloids – no slouches in taking advantage of opportunities to indulge in Beckham-mania – played this latest episode in the Beckham–Ferguson soap opera for all it was worth. Not for the first time Beckham had appeared to well and truly get his own back on Fergie.

To say that Ferguson's decision to part company with Beckham was a brave one is an understatement. Beckham, who celebrated his 28th birthday in May 2003, is still a top-class player. United's chief executive, Peter Kenyon, has said that the transfer was prompted mainly by the uncertainty over whether Beckham would be prepared to commit himself to the club beyond the remaining two years of his existing contract. Kenyon explained: 'Normally, when a player has two years left on his contract we either renew his deal or accept that it might be best he move on elsewhere, allowing us to earn a fee on his sale. What does not make sense for the club is to let top players leave at the end of their contract on a free transfer. In David's case our approach to his advisers about extending his current deal in mid-May [at a time when his relationship with Fergie was at its lowest ebb] did not meet with an immediate positive response.' However, there is no evidence to suggest that Beckham's emotional attachment to United had declined and that he would not have been happy to extend his agreement had Ferguson made the right noises.

Other factors also made it difficult for outsiders to get their heads round Beckham's departure. The club he moved to – Real Madrid, for £25 million – are United's biggest European rivals. Amazement at this part of the story was allied to the opinion that United had treated Beckham badly. Gordon Taylor, chief executive of the Professional Footballers' Association, hit out at United's action in initially striking a provisional £30-million deal for Beckham with Barcelona, apparently without Beckham's knowledge and when the man from whom they received the bid – Barcelona's presidential candidate Joan Laporta – was not yet in a position to sanction it. Taylor claimed that Beckham was being treated like 'a second-hand car'. He said: 'It's not a way I'd like to be treated – it's not the way I would want any of my members to be treated. He's one of our finest members and he has given Manchester United so much loyal service. It's harping back to the bad old days, when it was just a matter for a club to decide whether a player goes or stays. You wouldn't want to sell your second-hand car in such a way, never mind one of your finest assets. I just do not understand why and for what purpose United have allowed themselves to become involved in an election for the presidency of a club in Spain. [The promise of adding Beckham to Barcelona's team was Laporta's trump card in seeking election.] It's pure exploitation of David and for Manchester United to be part of it, I find quite [incredible].'

Publicly Beckham kept a dignified silence on the issue, and, even when he eventually completed his Real Madrid move, any temptation to increase his lead over Fergie in the public opinion polls was resisted. 'There are highs and lows with your boss in any job,' he said. 'He gave me the chance to play for United and that is something I will always appreciate.'

This diplomacy sits comfortably with Beckham's placid nature. But then, he hardly needed to put the boot in on Fergie, when there were so many others willing to do it. In one interview, Beckham's 'heartbroken' father Ted, who had previously revealed that his son and Ferguson had not spoken to each other for two months, said he was 'choked' about the move to Spain. 'I feel choked that he is going and the way he's had to go. David does not want to go. He's being forced out.'

All of this accentuated the hero and villain roles that were quickly assigned to Beckham and Ferguson respectively. Fergie was bound to be cast in the role of baddie. He lacks Beckham's charm, and while his success has brought him enormous respect in England, he has rarely attracted any great degree of national warmth and affection. Ferguson's chances of being widely applauded over his stance with Beckham were always going to be minimal.

The debate about the relationship and the pair's parting of the ways – highlighted by massive media coverage throughout Europe and beyond – spilled into every corner of society. The general consensus saw Beckham as a 'national institution', and branded his move from England a 'tragedy'. Considerable ill-feeling was directed at Ferguson over the Beckham issue – at least by football outsiders. The respected investigative journalist Tom Bower was particularly outspoken about him in an article for the *Guardian*.

Bower claimed that Ferguson was 'jealous' of the favourable publicity Beckham attracts. Among his observations were: 'Football is the vehicle for prima donnas and few are more self-preening than Ferguson. . . . His [Beckham's] fame and £50m fortune from sponsorship challenges his manager. . . . Ferguson is contemptuous of the England team and shows no concern that Beckham, the captain, will be exiled abroad. . . . Brazenly, Ferguson treats Beckham as a commodity, immune to sentiment. Beckham is more than a footballer. He represents the best of British youth . . . his imminent departure provokes unedifying but fundamental questions about British football and about modern Britain.'

But it takes two to tango and the spectacular falling out of step can be explained in a number of other ways. The most obvious factor, apart from the differences between their personalities, is the 33-year age gap. In terms of the social and economic generations in which they were born and raised, and in which their mentalities were shaped, they are from alien worlds. This is particularly noticeable in relation to their professional football careers.

The 61-year-old Fergie is often described as a 'real' football man. The tag relates to his adherence to the traditional values of the British game, and more specifically to the values that the great managers and players of his generation embraced. By that criterion, real football men eat, sleep and breathe the game – and they have no problem at all in relating to Bill Shankly's football-is-more-important-than-life-or-death philosophy. Real football men, as Fergie would recognise them, are not interested in being celebrities. They do not wear sarongs or Alice bands. Unlike Beckham, they would die of embarrassment if they were regarded as gay icons.

The relationship between the two men is touched on in a book about Beckham by Professor Ellis Cashmore, the lecturer for a University of Staffordshire degree course on the player's appeal and its cultural significance. He points out that the form of masculinity Beckham presents – 'sweet-natured, caring, nurturing, doting, full of soft, humanizing touches' – is far from the norm in the macho world of professional football. As Cashmore says, the conflict between Beckham and Ferguson was that of 'twenty-first-century New Man and traditional football man'. Referring to the dispute between the two men when Beckham missed training to look after his sick son, Cashmore said that Ferguson's 'world' during his upbringing was not one in which wives or womenfolk had much say in their men's lives. 'The idea that even a family man could skip training to attend to his child while his wife was somewhere else was too much [for Ferguson] to countenance. It must have contradicted Ferguson's definition of manliness.'

Ferguson, the son of a shipyard worker and a factory worker, and Beckham, the son of a gas-fitter and a hairdresser, both had disciplined, caring upbringings. But Fergie would possibly argue that the environment in which he was raised was tougher, and more conducive to building strong character. Beckham was brought up with his two sisters in a semi in Chingford, east London; Fergie was raised with his brother Martin in a tenement (with no bathroom) in the Glasgow ship-building area of Govan alongside the River Clyde.

Of his own childhood Ferguson has said: 'Nobody could say it was the gentlest environment. Most of the boys [he grew up with] ended up in jail or with drink problems.' Ferguson, for all his success and wealth, has never allowed himself to lose sight of these roots. Thanks to the influence of his father who ensured he always kept his feet on the ground, Fergie derives considerable pride from them. Indeed, the principle of individuals remaining true to themselves, their upbringing and their culture is a sensitive subject for him. I was once given an insight into this during the early phase of his managerial career in Scotland. An interview about international football provoked a bitter Fergie tirade directed against some members of the Scotland team who had left the country to join English clubs. He felt that the increase in their earnings on the other side of the border and their more glamorous lifestyles had had a negative effect on them. To Fergie, their clothes, cars and the way they conducted themselves on their trips back to Scotland indicated that they had become 'flash'. It seems likely that this word might have crossed Fergie's mind on a number of occasions in relation to Posh and Becks. But what would Fergie have given to possess the England captain's footballing ability when he was a player?

Fergie, a centre-forward, readily concedes that he was not among the most technically gifted of strikers. But thanks to his excellent knowledge of the game and single-mindedness, he did gain representative honours. He was selected for the

Scottish League against the English League, and in the summer of 1967 he was part of the Scotland squad for a world tour taking in matches in Israel, Hong Kong, Australia, New Zealand and Canada. He played in seven of the matches and scored 10 goals. But a Thierry Henry he wasn't.

The attributes for which he was best known were his determination and his combativeness. He was no shrinking violet when it came to personal duels of a gladiatorial nature – he could trade kicks and elbow digs with anybody. He was also headstrong and impetuous: his six-club career, which started in 1961 at Queen's Park (where he combined playing with serving an apprenticeship as a toolmaker) and ended in 1974 at Ayr United, could best be described as erratic.

Little wonder, then, that the players against whom Fergie's anger is most often directed include those who waste their talent through not applying themselves properly.

In club football Fergie's greatest claim to fame came in 1963, when he was playing for

St Johnstone. He became the first player ever to score a hat-trick against Rangers at Ibrox. Rangers were also involved in Fergie's most shattering experience as a player – an experience that was to have a major bearing on his approach as a manager.

Rangers, to a great extent the Manchester United of Scottish football, were his local club – the Ibrox stadium was within easy walking distance of his home and overlooked his school. Fergie had supported the club since he was a small boy; and when they signed him from Dunfermline in 1969 for a then record fee of £65,000, it was the most thrilling moment of his life. As he has said: 'How could I forget those schooldays playing on the Ibrox School pitch with the great man himself – the Rangers manager Bill Struth – watching from his window in the stadium? Often I made sure I was playing at outside left in one half and at outside right in the other so that he had every chance of seeing me. I was only 10 years of age, but I was convinced that he had to sign me immediately.'

As a boy, of course, Beckham had the same feelings about Manchester United. But while almost all of Beckham's Old Trafford hopes and aspirations were realised, Ferguson had a rather different story to tell about his time with Rangers. In his autobiography, the title of the chapter covering his three years at Ibrox says it all: 'Shattered Dreams'. In his first season he was their top scorer with 23 goals. But by the time he left – for Falkirk in the Second Division – he had been demoted to the third team and was training with the reserves.

Ferguson was not helped by the fact that the man who signed him for Rangers, Scot Symon, was sacked by the club and replaced a few months later by Davie White, a less ardent Fergie admirer, during that first season. Moreover, Fergie has claimed that he was a victim of religious bigotry. Sectarianism has always been a disturbingly potent part of the rivalry between Rangers and Celtic, and in the 1960s, Rangers' refusal to sign Catholic players was a declared policy. Ferguson – a Protestant – insists that his marriage to a Catholic caused one powerful behind-the-scenes figure at Ibrox to work against him there.

But of all his unhappy moments at Rangers, none got to him as much as being made the scapegoat for their surprise defeat by Celtic in the 1967 Scottish Cup Final. Ferguson partly owed his place in the side to an injury to Colin Stein, the centre-forward Rangers had bought from Hibernian for £100,000 before the start of the season. Even before the game Fergie had good cause to wish he had been injured himself. He was not enamoured of Rangers' tactical plan, nor of the instruction that he should be the one to mark Billy McNeill, Celtic's captain and centre-half, at Celtic corners.

This idea had been put forward by the Rangers' centre-half, Ronnie McKinnon, who had admitted that he did not feel confident about coping with McNeill's heading ability. Fergie, who was shorter than McNeill, suggested that it should be a dual responsibility, with him challenging McNeill (at least making it difficult for him to connect with the ball) and McKinnon attacking the ball. The plan misfired spectacularly after only a couple of minutes, when the wily McNeill lost Fergie (and exposed McKinnon's fallability at the same time, according to Fergie) to head Celtic into the lead. Celtic went on to win 4–0, and it was the beginning of the end for Ferguson at Rangers.

In truth, Fergie became a victim of his own headstrong, impetuous streak. He has admitted that there were a few occasions in his playing career when it worked against him. It did so at Rangers because, in his determination to move, he overlooked the possibility of bouncing back into prominence there under a different manager. While Fergie was in the process of pulling down the curtain on his Ibrox career, it was clear that Davie White was unlikely to be there much longer either.

In fact White was sacked shortly after Fergie's departure. This, though, has done nothing to help Fergie come to terms with the way Rangers treated him. It left a wound which has never totally healed. In a TV documentary about the factors that drive him, the accomplished sports writer Hugh McIlvanney, who ghosted Ferguson's autobiography and is a close friend, put it this way: 'Alex is cursed with a wonderful memory. Alex will remember all of it [his Rangers career] with a pretty ferocious clarity, and he will still be capable of reacting decades on. I think what happened to Alex at Ibrox did stoke fires that were already pretty fierce in him – fires to succeed. It is a minor agony, perhaps, in the broad part of his life, but he doesn't really feel it as minor. He regards it as a disturbing theme.'

It is tempting to suggest that Fergie has a chip on his shoulder. And it is no coincidence that most of his teams (if not all) have occasionally appeared to have chips on their shoulders too.

In striving to get the best out of teams, Ferguson has always been a great believer in giving his players what he describes as a 'common cause'. To Ferguson, no common cause is stronger than the sense of being unfairly treated. Getting a group of players to believe that the outside world is against them, or considers them inferior in some way, is a motivational skill at which Fergie excels. Not infrequently he has even been happy to stoke up dressing-room animosity so that he himself becomes the common cause against which the players unite.

The common enemy method worked particularly well at Aberdeen, where Ferguson's team-talks for the key matches against Rangers and Celtic invariably revolved around the power and influence of those two clubs, and the extent to which clubs like Aberdeen were regarded as important only in terms of making up numbers. To reinforce his anti-Old Firm message, Fergie was particularly fond of setting up the attitude of Scottish League referees and the Celtic–Rangers-obsessed west of Scotland media as examples. As a result, the Aberdeen team could always be relied upon to take the field with a point to prove – so wound up, in fact, that a number of their Old Firm battles were not for the squeamish.

It is difficult to believe that players keep on responding to Fergie's rhetoric, but Craig Brown, the former Scotland manager and one of his closest friends in the game, says: 'Fergie is very clever. He perhaps does not come over very well on TV – I know some people say that he is not very articulate, for example. But believe me, this is misleading.' Gordon Strachan, who played for Fergie at Aberdeen and Manchester United, adds: 'You knew what he was trying to do in his Aberdeen team-talks – that it was a bit of an act – but he was still able to get you to respond to it.'

It was perhaps only to be expected of a team managed by someone with Ferguson's personality that Aberdeen, unlike many other sides, were in no way intimidated by Old Firm reputations in their matches against Rangers and Celtic. Instead of setting their sights on just containing them and avoiding a hiding, Aberdeen went for their opponents' throats. Having overcome the psychological barrier that had prevented other sides from getting the better of the Old Firm, Aberdeen were able to make a habit of it.

Thus Aberdeen – after many years in which Celtic and Rangers had exerted an iron grip on the major trophies in Scotland – became the country's outstanding team of the 1980s. And under Ferguson it was not just in Scottish football that Aberdeen excelled, pushing Rangers and Celtic into the background. His management style also steered them to that glorious 2–1 victory over Real Madrid in the 1983 European Cup Winners' Cup – the last European trophy won by a Scottish team.

His motivational approach has also been in evidence at Manchester United. Creating a common cause there has been made easy for him by the widespread resentment of the club's massive financial resources and arrogant persona. No doubt, if Fergie had his way, they would take to the field with the message: 'Nobody likes us, we don't care' emblazoned on their jerseys.

However, as David Beckham has illustrated, some footballers have less cause to carry a chip on the shoulder than others.

Chapter Two

The Courtship

One of the most famous football adverts of all time is a Nike billboard poster referring to Eric Cantona's success at Manchester United. It said: '1966 was a great year for English football. It was the year Eric was born.' But 1986 was not a bad one either. It was the year when Ferguson and Beckham started on the path that would bring them together.

It was in November 1986, when United were second from bottom in the old First Division, that Ferguson became their manager, taking over from Ron Atkinson. The following month, the 11-year-old Beckham became the centre of attention at Old Trafford by winning the final of a schoolboys' soccer skills competition there.

Beckham, like his father Ted, was a United supporter – much to the irritation of his paternal grandfather, a Tottenham fan. Ted Beckham had formed his attachment to United in the 1960s and almost from the moment David was born he was subjected to two indoctrination campaigns. 'My parents used to buy me a United kit, whereas my granddad bought me a Tottenham one,' Beckham said. 'To keep them both happy, I would wear Tottenham shorts and a United top.'

But Beckham, whose bedroom wall was adorned with pictures of Manchester United stars – especially his idol, Bryan Robson – was never in any doubt about which club inspired his football fantasies. The area in which he was brought up is very much Tottenham-fan territory. But on his daily journey to school he felt no compunction about wearing his United shirt over his uniform. He even wore it at Tottenham during the period he trained there.

The skills that made the young Beckham stand

out like a beacon in his local teams – starting with an Under-8s Enfield District League side called Ridgeway Rovers, for whom he scored 101 goals in three seasons – were the result of more than natural ability. There are millions of boys who fantasise about careers as professional football stars but few are prepared to work as hard as Beckham did to make their dreams a reality. The most distinct thread running through the recollections of those who knew Beckham as a schoolboy player is his desire to perfect his ball-playing techniques. Almost every spare moment was spent practising them under the guidance of his father. Ted Beckham, a Sunday League player who worked as a gas-fitter, was determined that if his son failed to do better in football than he had, it wouldn't be because David lacked a proper grasp of the fundamentals.

All this, combined with Beckham's love of Manchester United, led him to enrol in one of Bobby Charlton's Soccer Schools, the coaching camps set up some 25 years ago by the

Manchester United director – and, of course, former United and England forward. This resulted in Beckham's appearance on the pitch at Old Trafford at the age of 11.

Beckham had heard about the schools from TV when they were featured on *Blue Peter*. He was particularly intrigued to learn that the Charlton set-up encompassed a nationwide TSB-sponsored soccer skills competition, for which the first prize was a one-week trip to Spain to meet the Barcelona manager Terry Venables and his players.

The £125 it cost to enrol in a Charlton school, in this instance one in the Manchester area, proved to be money exceptionally well spent. No fewer than 5,000 boys entered the competition, but Beckham was in a class of his own. Making the skill tests look easy, Beckham finished top of his coaching group to clinch a place in that Old Trafford final – and, in a field of around 100 boys from all over the United Kingdom, he comfortably came out on top again. A 16-year-old was second and a 13-year-old third.

Beckham was a star pupil at the school again in 1987 and 1988. On its official website Bryn Cooper, the then course director, recalls: 'David had tremendous ability as a young boy. Such was his ability that in 1988 he was transferred from the 13-year-old age group to an older one. Despite this, David still achieved the highest skills score. In addition to his natural ability, David displayed a fantastic work ethic and a great deal of determination, which meant he was continually practising his individual skills. It was clearly evident to the coaches at Bobby Charlton Soccer Schools that David was completely focused on becoming a professional footballer.'

Charlton certainly felt that to be true. He has said: 'If David has a secret, it is that he is so hungry to be the best. That is the quality I first saw in him when he was a schoolboy. Probably, I saw a lot of myself in him as a boy, with his love of the game and overwhelming desire to be a professional footballer. He is a perfectionist.'

So it was little wonder that United signed him

as a trainee aged 16 in July 1991 and as a professional in January 1993, when he was still four months short of his 18th birthday.

As a teenager with star potential, Beckham was in good company at Old Trafford. He was one of a number of exciting youth team players who were all bursting through the ranks towards first-team places at virtually the same time. Ferguson could take a lot of the credit for this, if only because of the determination with which he had set about improving United's youth system when he took over. As he has said: 'It [a crop of outstanding young players] tends to go in cycles, but that does not mean that you can afford not to work exceptionally hard at it.'

That hard work brought hugely impressive results at Aberdeen. 'The first eight players I signed all made the first team, and six of them went on to represent Scotland, either at full or Under-21 level,' Ferguson said. The results were even more spectacular at United, where Fergie was fortunate enough to find himself with the biggest and most impressive collection of up-

and-coming youngsters since the club's renowned 'Busby Babes' of the 1950s.

Beckham was fortunate, too. He now found himself in a team who could further enhance his ability. In United's FA Youth Cup-winning side of 1992, his teammates in the final against Crystal Palace included Ryan Giggs (the oldest of the group at 18½ and a player who had already established himself as a first-team regular), Gary Neville and Nicky Butt. In the 1993 final, when they lost to Leeds United, Phil Neville and Paul Scholes were added to the list.

For all the plaudits he attracted at youth and reserve-team levels, though, Beckham's challenge for first-team football was not as dynamic as many anticipated. Part of the reason for this lay in Ferguson's doubts about his physical and mental strength. Eric Harrison, the former United youth team coach who is widely acknowledged as having played as big a part as anyone in the rise of players like Beckham, has said: 'David had to be nursed along a bit between the ages of 16 and 17 because his physique was changing dramatically. He literally shot up in size. The stamina was still there – believe you me, David can run all day – but the strength was not. He was frustrated at not progressing as fast as some of the other lads. As always, I was constantly talking to the boys one-to-one and I think these chats helped David. He has always been a little sensitive but a brilliant lad to work with.'

In September 1992, Fergie did select Beckham for his first-team debut at 17. He was chosen as a substitute for the Coca-Cola Cup tie at Brighton. Beckham, who had not expected to play, came on and did reasonably well in a 1–1 draw, but it was not until the first half of the 1994/95 season that he was given further first-team opportunities – against Port Vale (twice) and Newcastle United in the Coca-Cola Cup, and in December in the European Champions League tie against Turkey's Galatasaray, in which he scored his first United goal.

The fact that Fergie and his coaching staff still felt Beckham needed some toughening up –

some more first-team experience in an environment that would subject him to the less glamorous aspects of professional football in England – was confirmed by the decision in March 1995 to loan him to Third Division Preston. Such moves often prove to be the beginning of the end for players with top-level pretensions, so the messages this decision relayed to Beckham cannot have been very encouraging. But the culture shock of Preston – where he was introduced to such non-Manchester United habits as having to wash his own kit, and where some of his opponents appeared to relish the sight of blood – proved no problem to him. Preston's manager, Gary Peters, was later quoted as saying: 'There was no questioning his ability, but they [Fergie and Co. at United] did not believe he got stuck in enough. I was a bit worried that David would struggle with the physical side. At first, I had to bully and cajole him a bit. But David soon got the message that he had to mix it with the hard nuts and he learned very quickly.'

These early reservations about Beckham seem absurd in the light of some of his clashes with opponents in Manchester United and England matches. In addition to the yellow and red cards he has collected, his on-field conduct once prompted the Football Association's compliance officer, Graham Bean, to demand a warning meeting with him. As for his physique, Eric Harrison points out: 'When David started to get stronger, he really blossomed. We now had a midfield player who had all the skill in the world, who could run for fun and had the physique to go with it. Quickly he had been transformed from a small, skinny lad to a six-footer with broad shoulders. We were now seeing the David Beckham that I had always visualised.'

After returning to United from Preston (following five Preston matches in which he had scored one goal direct from a corner and another from one of those trademark Exocet-missile-type free kicks), Beckham at last made his Premiership debut against Leeds at Old

Trafford on 2 April 1995. He was given the chance because of an injury to Andrei Kanchelskis, but his performance in the 1–1 draw prompted further reservations about his abilities. The match report in the *Guardian* said: 'Although the 19-year-old Beckham did well, he could not be expected to provide the service that [Andy] Cole has come to expect from Kanchelskis.'

In a sense this was true. Kanchelskis was like an Olympic sprinter, all power and pace. Unlike Beckham, he was more of a winger than a midfielder and in taking on defenders he was able repeatedly to beat them clearly enough to get the ball into the middle from on or near the goal-line. But there is more than one way to produce good crosses for strikers, and Beckham, slower than Kanchelskis but a superior striker of the ball, provided the perfect alternative. So when Kanchelskis was sold to Everton for £5 million in the 1995 close-season – leaving at the same time as other established stars including Paul Ince to Inter Milan and Mark

Hughes to Chelsea – Fergie had no hesitation in installing Beckham as his replacement.

At that time Fergie was smarting at United's being pipped to the 1995 Championship by Blackburn, a failure he attributed to complacency among his players and to the fact that he had not been given the cash to bring in newcomers who could take the team to a higher level. He was convinced that a major shake-up was necessary. As a result, in addition to Beckham's presence in the team for the opening Premiership match of the 1995/96 season at Aston Villa, the line-up also included similarly inexperienced ex-youth team players Gary and Phil Neville, Nicky Butt and Paul Scholes.

This team sheet staggered a number of people in the game. Few managers – and especially those at big clubs with the transfer-market spending money to sign established stars – would have had the bottle to do what Fergie did. Young players can be erratic and his decision to chuck so many in at the Premiership deep end at the same time was viewed in some quarters as a recipe for disaster. This was certainly the opinion of the former Liverpool and Scotland defender Alan Hansen – an opinion he shared with millions in his capacity as one of BBC TV's leading soccer pundits. United were beaten 3–1 by Villa that day and on *Match of the Day* Hansen proclaimed: 'You never win anything with kids.'

But with Beckham and Co. – 'Fergie's Fledgelings' as they were dubbed – going from strength to strength, and winning everything but the proverbial kitchen sink, Hansen has never been allowed to live that statement down. That United proved him wrong so spectacularly was not just down to the talent of the young players and Fergie's management skills. It also owed much to the guidance and inspiration they were given by the senior professionals around them – notably a Frenchman by the name of Eric Cantona.

No single footballer has ever proved more important to Manchester United than Cantona. Indeed, in assessing the factors that helped make the relationship between Beckham and Ferguson so successful, Cantona is as good a starting-point as any.

The 1992 signing of Cantona was very much a turning point for Ferguson in his efforts to produce a Championship-winning team. Until that point Fergie had not done badly in his six years at Old Trafford. It was certainly more than satisfactory for United to finish in 11th place in the table in the 1986/87 season in view of their low position when he arrived in November and his misgivings about the standard of discipline in the squad he inherited. He was particularly concerned about the drinking habits of Bryan Robson, Paul McGrath and Norman Whiteside, who were regarded as his key players.

Though United were runners-up to Liverpool in the 1987/88 title race, albeit by an emphatic nine-point margin, they finished 11th again in the 1988/89 season. At this stage they didn't look like winning any trophies at all, let alone the Championship, and as their underwhelming results and performances continued in the opening half of the 1989/90 season (they were to finish 13th in the table this time) speculation about Fergie's position became increasingly negative. By the time of United's FA Cup third round tie at Nottingham Forest in January 1990 – when it was clear that this was the only competition they had a realistic chance of winning – it was widely felt that a defeat would signal the end of the Old Trafford road for him.

United, though, scrambled a 1–0 win with a goal by Mark Robins, and went on to get their hands on the trophy by overcoming Crystal Palace in the final. The following season, Fergie reinforced his position as manager by steering United to victory over Barcelona in the European Cup Winners' Cup Final.

But the trophy Manchester United wanted most was the Championship and securing it had become little short of an obsession for everyone connected with the club. After all, the last time United had won the title was back in 1967. For a club of their stature, this record of failure was a source of infinite embarrassment. So imagine the sense of disappointment that engulfed United in the 1991/92 season when they had the title in their grasp only to be pipped at the post by Leeds United.

Cantona was a member of that winning Leeds team, adding touches of flair to their generally straightforward brand of football as a substitute over the last lap. Just over six months later, Ferguson decided to buy him for £1.2 million – it was arguably the best decision he has ever made.

Leeds were prepared to offload Cantona because they were unable to provide him with the sort of stage he required to give of his best. Indeed, having been signed initially by Leeds on loan from Nîmes, Cantona's emergence as a cult figure among the Elland Road faithful was misleading. On the field, he never truly looked comfortable in the Leeds set-up.

The biggest target for his frustration, beyond the manager, Howard Wilkinson, was Leeds centre-forward Lee Chapman. 'We played a very direct game, and I was the target man,'

Chapman once explained. 'The ball was played quite early up to me, and people fed off me. Eric really prefers to play between the midfield and the forwards. But we did not play like that so he tended to be overlooked all the time.' It has been claimed that this prompted Cantona to put pressure on Wilkinson to drop Chapman. The latter, recalling the shock of being left out of the team for a match against Manchester City, has said: 'I could not do something like that [to a fellow player] but Eric is very single-minded, and if he isn't in control of the situation and if it isn't all revolving around Eric, he finds it difficult to play second-fiddle.'

Leeds would have to have changed their whole system, their whole mentality, in order to accommodate Cantona properly. When it came to giving the Frenchman the scope to express fully his brilliant attacking skills, not to mention his arrogance, Manchester United were a different proposition altogether. United's style of play was more individualistic. Moreover,

Cantona's self-confidence and sense of authority were particularly important to United at that time, given the psychological effect of their traumatic Championship experience the previous season. If ever there was a big personality who could dominate matches and infect teammates and fans alike with his own brand of self-belief, it was Cantona.

'Eric was born to play for Manchester United,' Ferguson said. 'Some players with respected and established reputations are cowed and broken by the size of this club and its expectations. Not Eric. He swaggered in, stuck his chest out, raised his head and surveyed everything as if to say: "I'm Cantona. How big are you? Are you big enough for me?"'

Because of Cantona's temperament, his need to be seen as a man apart, many predicted that his relationship with Ferguson would turn into a football marriage from hell. But strange as it might seem – and it must certainly have seemed strange to those who have felt the full force of Fergie's authoritarian approach over the years –

the manager was willing to compromise in Cantona's case.

In his biography of Cantona, Ian Ridley relates the story of a United celebration party hosted by the city's Lord Mayor. 'All were in club blazers, grey flannels, white shirts and official red and black ties – except one. "What are you going to do about that, gaffer?" one senior player asked of Alex Ferguson, pointing at this lofty figure wearing some kind of tunic top and generally dressed for one of the city's trendy evening venues. Ferguson simply smiled.' In his autobiography Mark Hughes wrote: 'The manager had to stretch a few principles to accommodate a Frenchman who is his own man and who obviously has had his problems conforming with certain requirements. Alex Ferguson did not exactly re-write the rule book, but he treated him differently and explained to the rest of us that he was a special player requiring special treatment.'

Such stories – and other instances where Ferguson might have given the impression of double standards – will not have been lost on Beckham when the manager was taking exception to his acts of non-conformity. But neither Beckham nor any other United player in the supporting cast at the Old Trafford Cantona show would begrudge the Frenchman his place in the spotlight.

Technically, Cantona brought a whole new dimension to United's play. His free role in the 'hole' behind the strikers made it difficult for the opposition to decide who should mark him. Big, powerfully built and breathtakingly skilful, he was able to drop deep and repeatedly set up chances with ingenious passes through the defence, or to get on the end of moves and score himself. Above all, he was the conductor of the orchestra.

The music was uplifting right from the start. In the season of Cantona's arrival, United made up for the title blow that Leeds inflicted upon them by achieving the Championship–FA Cup double. Two seasons later, with Beckham and the other young guns supporting him, they did it again.

Beckham has always maintained that Cantona was his No. 1 role model at United. No player in his right mind would want to follow many aspects of the explosive side of Cantona's character, but on the basis of purely football criteria, Beckham was in awe of him. 'He is the best I have ever played with,' he once said. 'A great guy – one day I would like to be as charismatic as him.'

Another factor in Cantona's influence on Beckham, and on the other players who started their first-team careers when he was at Old Trafford, was his professionalism behind the scenes. Players with his natural ability are not usually known for working particularly hard on their techniques in training. They tend to take the view that they don't need to work hard. But not Cantona.

Speaking at an FA coaches conference in 1997, Ferguson said: 'When Cantona first came to the club, we used to finish training at mid-day. On his first day, when the session had finished, he came up to me and asked if he could have two players to practise with. I shouted to Eric Harrison [the youth team coach] and asked for two players. He said: "What for?" I said: "To practise with, you stupid bugger." The jungle drums began to beat and soon everyone was dying to join in. Eric has a million faults, but the example he set for the other players in training was tremendous. That's the biggest thing he did for this club.'

It was fitting that Cantona should wear the United No. 7 shirt, the team number worn by previous Old Trafford legends George Best and Bryan Robson. When Beckham (previously United's No. 10) was handed that shirt following Cantona's departure from Old Trafford and retirement from football in 1997, it was arguably the greatest compliment that Fergie ever paid him. Beckham proved worthy of it, even though his role in the team and style of play were generally less noticeable than those of his illustrious No. 7 predecessors.

Of course, it is open to doubt whether Ferguson felt that Beckham lived up to his

No. 7 shirt as much as the player's admirers did – especially towards the end of his career at Old Trafford. Insiders claim that although Ferguson admired Beckham's ability, the honour of being given Cantona's number did not encourage the player to develop as much as Fergie had hoped.

When reviewing his squad after United's 1999 treble success, Ferguson was quoted as saying: 'The possibilities are endless. Most of those lads are still maturing as players. The United side of 1994 was full of strong people, strong personalities. Robson, Bruce, Cantona, Hughes – they influenced other people with their strength. This team has developed along those lines and that same strength is coming out. Keane, Stam, Schmeichel; they influence people. David Beckham influences the game. Eventually he will influence the others. And then, we will have some player, won't we?' Four years later, it is reasonable to suggest that if Ferguson felt Beckham was now in that category, or could still be expected to attain it, he would not have let him go.

For his part, Beckham has always wanted to play in the central midfield area. A number of players in the more restrictive wide midfield areas have added new dimensions to their careers through switching – one notable post-war example is John Giles, who started his career at Manchester United at outside-right but moved to Leeds where he became one of the most influential of all central midfield generals. Opinions are divided on whether Beckham and United would have benefited from such a change. But his cause was not helped by the fact that he remained so effective where he was.

Beckham is looked upon as the best striker of a ball in the world. The spectacular aspect of this talent is, of course, his ability to score direct from free kicks – a characteristic that stems partly from the amount of time he has spent practising the art by firing the ball at car tyres suspended from the crossbar. Quite apart from the accuracy and power of his kicks, Beckham seems to be able to make the ball almost sing and dance in these situations. Other aspects of his game that represented major attacking weapons for United were his corners and crosses.

Over the years, the chances he has created have been well documented through his consistently high placing in the Opta Index statistical analysis of players' performance. To Opta Index followers, it will have come as no surprise that Beckham got in the highest number of crosses and achieved the greatest accuracy in 2002/03 Premiership matches. In the circumstances, Ferguson's unwillingness to sacrifice this aspect of Beckham's play was understandable.

In the 4–4–2 system that Ferguson has favoured in the past, the Beckham position as the widest of the midfield quartet is far from easy. Because the player is often called upon to perform virtually as a right full-back one moment and as a right-winger the next, it is a position that requires a lot of stamina. There can be no doubt that Beckham has it. Middlesbrough's manager Steve McClaren, who was once Ferguson's Manchester United assistant and was also Sven-Goran Eriksson's right-hand man in the England set-up, had this to say when interviewed about that Beckham World Cup display against Greece. Noting that Beckham had run more than 10 miles during the game, he said: 'He just has that natural kind of fitness, the kind you are born with. He has been like that as long as I have known him. He does not rely on dieticians or fads, although you can tell he lives well. The one thing I would say is that to be fit, your lifestyle has to be perfect. You cannot survive on burgers and chips. His performances show that he leads an exemplary lifestyle.'

McClaren talked about Beckham's running power in training, especially when he is taking the 'bleep' test. This is an intense fitness competition in which players run a set distance, and on hearing the bleep, run back to their starting position. The time between the bleeps becomes gradually shorter, and the player is out once he can't reach the other side before the bleep goes. McClaren recalled: 'I remember [at

Manchester United] giving him a rest from the game for a week to ten days, and the day he returned to training happened to be our fitness test day. After ten days of doing practically nothing, he came and did the bleep test. Well, he beat everybody out of sight. We actually had to tell him to stop because he was the only one left and would have just kept running and running. That sums him up. When you put his fitness together with his enthusiasm for the game, and his determination, you get the package you saw in the Greece match.'

Another right-side midfielder in English football who attracted such professional praise was Trevor Steven, the Everton and England player of the 1980s. He said: 'In the attacking sense, the role was a little easier for me than it is for David because I had more of a change of pace – I could run away from people with the ball whereas David has to do it more through passing. But one way in which I can easily relate to him is that, apart from the work he gets through, he shows a lot of discipline.

'That discipline really is crucial in this role because, being out wide, you can go for so long without getting the ball. OK, you can move inside, you can go looking for it. But there are limitations there as well because of the need for a team to keep its shape. In any system, once a player is caught out of position, you are done for. There is no doubt that in the centre, you get more opportunities to do different things. It can be so frustrating [on the right or left] when you have not touched the ball for a while. Then when you do get it, you feel under pressure to do something special. It is so easy to get too uptight.'

The sense of being on the periphery of the action, with not enough scope to show all that he can do, helps explain why Beckham has derived so much joy from his free-kick goals. Once asked whether he took free kicks because he wanted to be the centre of attention, Beckham replied: 'I like to be looked at in that way. I like people to look at me for my football and think "Wow".'

After Beckham established himself as a United first-team regular at the start of the 1995/96 season, that was precisely what most people in English football were thinking at the beginning of the following season as they watched his astonishing goal in a 3–0 win at Wimbledon. Towards the end, with United 2–0 up, Beckham received possession just inside his own half; he spotted Wimbledon keeper Neil Sullivan some way off his line. At that stage United were just concentrating on retaining possession – they were coasting and saw no need to over-exert themselves with any attempt to increase the lead. But Beckham, epitomising the boldness (and maybe naivety) of most bright young footballers, hit a 55-yard shot over Sullivan's head and into the net.

That strike had a considerable influence on England manager Glenn Hoddle, who gave Beckham his international debut the following month in the World Cup qualifying tie against Moldova. Hoddle, likening Beckham's shot to the famous Pele strike from the half-way line which almost brought the Brazilian legend a goal against Czechoslovakia in the 1970 World Cup, said: 'David's goal elevated him [to the England team] a bit quicker than he might otherwise have been. He is a talented player and it took him a couple of rungs up the ladder quickly. That happens when you score special goals. People will remember them, not the simple tap-ins.' Beckham said: 'That goal was definitely a watershed for me. It did not change me as a person, but from a football point of view, I was suddenly looked at in a different way.'

Beckham's scoring record for United was 86 goals in around 400 games, but, of course, this figure was dwarfed by the number of goals he set up for others. In that respect, one of his most memorable games – and one that again showed how he relished any opportunity to have the last word in any dispute with Fergie – was the 2–1 European Champions League win over Juventus at Old Trafford in February 2003. It was his first game after the flying boot fracas, and he capped an excellent all-round performance by setting up both United goals. The second, when Beckham set up Ruud Van Nistelrooy with a remarkable long-range pass the like of which any American football quarter-back would have been proud, was worthy of the admission price alone.

Even more memorable was the part Beckham played in United's epic 2–1 triumph over Bayern Munich in the 1999 European Champions League Final in Barcelona. That victory allowed Fergie to realise his personal dream of emulating Sir Matt Busby's European Cup success with United in 1968.

Busby's United had slaughtered the opposition (Benfica) in extra time in the final. But this was a different story. Had it been a horse race, then United's win after falling behind to a goal after five minutes and looking off-colour for most of the match would surely have prompted a stewards' inquiry. In the aftermath of the victory, even Ferguson struggled to explain the result fully, other than suggesting that Bayern became too negative and that he found a good way to motivate his men at half-time when he told them: 'Just think about how you are going to feel if you lose – if the Cup is five yards away and you cannot touch it.'

Ferguson seemed to take exception to media comments that Beckham and Ryan Giggs, more important than ever to United in the absence of Roy Keane and Paul Scholes, did not play particularly well. In Beckham's case, Fergie pronounced: 'He was the star of the midfield show.' Not many outsiders saw it that way, but nobody could dispute that Beckham deserved some Fergie pats on the back.

No player worked harder than Beckham to put his manager in football Utopia. And the two agonisingly late goals with which United clinched victory from substitutes Teddy Sheringham and Ole Gunnar Solksjaer both stemmed from Beckham corners, the first of which he won himself. If Fergie has ever had cause to get down on his bended knees and thank David Beckham, this was the moment.

Chapter Three

Balance of Power

One of the most intriguing aspects of the control-freak element of Alex Ferguson's management style is that the vast majority of his counterparts in Britain no longer have the power to follow his lead. As the most successful manager of all time in England, Fergie has got himself into a position which is probably unique. Even at a club as big as Manchester United, Fergie reigns supreme.

This cannot be said of many others. They have generally become more vulnerable than ever, if only because clubs have grown more impatient – if not desperate – for success. On top of this, the most powerful and influential figures in football nowadays tend to be the chairmen, who take on a much more active part in the running of their clubs than their predecessors did, and the players, who have been given a licence to hold managers to ransom as a result of their vast basic salaries and the Bosman ruling.

These changes in the balance of power at British clubs have, indeed, seen most team bosses well and truly cut down in size. As Terry Venables has said: 'Managers have always been the meat in the sandwich at a football club. It is just that now we are being sliced thinner with every season that passes.'

As far as the chairmen are concerned, their emergence from the background stems from the fact that clubs have become multi-faceted business empires. This transformation, which has brought far more money into the game than can ever have been envisaged during the game's slump in the 1980s, began with Lord Justice Taylor's report into the 1989 Hillsborough disaster and his recommendation that clubs provide only seated accommodation at their grounds. The next step came in 1992, when the 22 clubs that made up the old First Division of the Football League – struggling to find the money needed to comply with the Taylor recommendation and with the carrot of a massive increase in television and sponsorship income dangling in front of them – broke away to form the Premiership.

Instead of having to share the television and sponsorship cash with the 70 clubs below them in the four-division Football League, the 22 Premiership teams could now keep it all for themselves. Having an elite league of their own put them more in control of their own destiny. They could move forward more quickly. As English football experienced an upsurge in popularity – thanks partly to England's performances in the 1990 World Cup Finals and the visual impact of Paul Gascoigne's tears of disappointment during the semi-final against Germany – the steps forward were particularly pronounced in the area of income derived from television coverage.

The Premiership started in 1992 with a five-year BSkyB–BBC agreement worth more than £250 million – a staggering figure, indeed, when set against the Football League's £44 million haul for its previous five-year agreement with ITV. The next four-year BSkyB–BBC deal was worth £743 million and each of the subsequent major contracts with television companies has taken income from this source into the £1 billion-plus bracket.

Since the formation of the Premiership, other major sources of club revenue have been developed, including corporate hospitality, merchandising and catering. In the most recent of its annual studies of football finances in England, Deloitte & Touche, referring to the 2001/02 season, revealed: 'Turnover [of Premiership clubs] increased seven-fold from 1991/2 [the last year of the old Division One] to £1,132 million in 2001/02. We estimate that Premiership clubs' income exceeded £1.25 billion in 2002/03.'

Football clubs have become vehicles for making pots of money and the inevitable result is that the attitude towards the game among the men who effectively own the clubs – in most cases the chairmen – has changed. At one time, they were men whose businesses rarely stretched beyond their club's home town or city, and they looked upon their position in football (which often stemmed from the inheritance of family shares) as little more than a prestigious hobby through which they could combine making a contribution to the community with impressing their friends and gaining some measure of public recognition. Now, the men at the helm of Premiership clubs – not least the dynamic, high-powered newcomers to the position – treat the role rather more seriously. It is not unusual for these figures to have their own offices at their club and to spend much of their time working there. As a result, the traditional terms of reference of the manager's job have become more limited, especially on the financial side.

In this respect, British football has followed the same pattern as the game in other major European football countries, where the managers – referred to as 'coaches' – are responsible only for purely football matters, such as training and team selection, and play little or no part in negotiations and decisions relating to players' transfer fees and contracts. The latter are the responsibilities of the club president or chairman. It is not unheard of for these men to buy players without the coach's knowledge.

One of the first clubs in England to initiate the continental system were Tottenham. It happened in the early 1980s when Keith Burkinshaw was manager and Irving Scholar (a chairman who could be described as a trail-blazer for his counterparts today) gained control at White Hart Lane. Burkinshaw, recalling a previous chairman, Sidney Wale, once told me: 'He was great for me. He used to come in on the Friday morning to pick up his match tickets for the next day, poke his head around my office door, and say: "Well, Keith, what's going on this week? Anything you want to tell me?" I would chat with him for a couple of minutes and then he'd say: "Right, must go – got my tickets to collect." That was all I saw of him. Outside things like ground improvements, he left me and Geoff Jones [then Spurs' club secretary] to run the club.'

Scholar, shrewdly recognising how the leading English clubs would be developed and realising that they needed to be broken down into departments run by specialists in particular fields, struggled to get Burkinshaw on his wavelength. It was hardly a chairman–manager match made in heaven. As Burkinshaw said: 'Instead of trying to adjust to his methods, I probably went the other way. I genuinely felt that if I gave him an inch [by agreeing to let Scholar run the whole financial show], he would take a mile [by attempting to run the football side as well].'

Burkinshaw, a stubborn, dyed-in-the-wool Yorkshireman if ever there was one, did have a point. It is hardly unusual for chairmen to reveal themselves as frustrated managers, if not players, at least within the privacy of their clubs. As Scholar has said: 'Like every fan at every game, they can all pick a better team or a better player to buy.'

The extent to which a manager is forced to take notice of his chairman in these matters tends to vary – some managers inevitably have greater autonomy than others. But some chairmen do give the impression that they think establishing a successful team is not quite the specialist art that managers claim it is; that managers have created something of a myth about their role.

Ron Noades, the former Wimbledon and Crystal Palace chairman who had a spell as a manager at Brentford, once told me: 'All the word "professional" means in football is that you earn a wage at it – it's not like being a chartered surveyor, is it? A lot of players who go on TV to analyse a match don't know what they are talking about. You could get people at boardroom level to go on and they would be able to discuss a game just as well, if not better.

They do not have the credibility; they are always being told they know nothing about football. But I know lots of directors far more knowledgeable about football than some of their players.'

Noades stopped short of claiming publicly that they are also more knowledgeable than some of their managers. 'I wouldn't say that because, if that were the case, they would have known eff-all to have appointed the manager in the first place.' But what he feels privately could be another matter.

The hands-on approach of today's club owners was brought into sharp focus again in the summer of 2003 with the Russian billionaire Roman Abramovich's sensational take-over of Chelsea. Having splashed out £140 million to buy the club and many millions more to fund the signing of exciting new players, Abramovich is clearly not intending just to sit back and admire his new train set. Abramovich talked to some sections of the media about his intention to have 'fun', and it seemed he was not just referring to his involvement in financial matters at Stamford Bridge. Talking about aspects of club life such as the buying and selling of players and team selection, he told the *Sun*: 'This is what the pleasure is all about, to participate in the game and the selection process. The coach will determine what areas are in need of new players. I will participate in that discussion and analysis.'

The extent to which he will do so remains to be seen. But it's easy to appreciate the remark made by John Barnwell, the chief executive of the League Managers' Association, about the terms of reference under which so many of his members now operate. He said: 'They have the responsibility [to get good results] without the power.'

Ferguson's relationships with his chairmen have been mixed. His dealings with Willie Todd at St Mirren became uneasy to say the least, and according to Fergie this was at least partly because of Todd's 'hunger for power'. Fergie was sacked by Todd for alleged breaches of his contract and then suffered the added ignominy of losing his industrial tribunal battle against the decision.

At Aberdeen, his relationship with Dick Donald, a delightful old character who had once been an Aberdeen goalkeeper and who had made his fortune from a family entertainment business comprising theatres, dance and bingo halls and cinemas, was well nigh perfect. Fergie has said that Donald, who helped to curb his impetuosity, was like a father to him. When they were still working together, Fergie said: 'His humility is the pervading factor at Pittodrie and the club operates from that base. As chairman, his approach is low key and his attitude is that people are employed to do certain jobs and should be left to do just that. I have always believed that the most important relationship at any football club is that between chairman and manager. I must say I have been more than fortunate to develop a close relationship with Dick Donald.'

Generally, he has not had too much to grumble about on that score at Old Trafford either. As a public limited company, United have to operate within the financial constraints of needing to make a profit each year to pay shareholders' dividends, and it is no secret that Ferguson has not always had the transfer-market spending money he has wanted, nor that this occasionally led him into conflict with United's former chairman and chief executive, Martin Edwards.

But because of his record Ferguson walks taller at his club than most managers do. Such is his stature in the game that even some fellow football professionals outside Manchester United are wary about doing anything which might turn him against them.

His success is particularly impressive because it has coincided with a sharp increase in so-called 'player power', and the managerial problems that have resulted from it in terms of getting the best out of teams.

Clubs themselves have done much to create those problems by forking out dangerously high percentages of their income on players' basic salaries. They have created a situation where footballers can quickly set themselves up financially for the rest of their lives without being particularly successful, while at the same time putting their club in financial trouble.

To many managers, Jean-Marc Bosman has even more to answer for. One outcome of the Belgian footballer's five-year legal dispute over the move he wanted to make from a club in his own country to one in France is that in 1995 players from European Union countries were given freedom of movement in accordance with the Treaty of Rome. This has been welcomed by British clubs, but they have not welcomed the other aspect of the Bosman case – most players can now change clubs at the end of their contracts without their new club having to pay their old one a transfer fee. Clubs can no longer hold a player's registration when his agreement has expired.

In view of his trade union background, Ferguson would seem the last person likely to take a dim view of the power wielded by these football 'workers'. In his days as an apprentice toolmaker, he led his young colleagues in an unofficial pay strike. He was in the thick of the Glasgow shipyard apprentices' strike of 1959, and was one of the most active members of the Scottish Professional Footballers' Association in its campaigns for better wages and pension rights for players.

However, Ferguson readily agrees that the pendulum has swung too far the other way. He has been quoted as saying: 'When I was a young player, unions were very necessary in all walks of life and we needed them to try to get a better deal for players – but those days have long gone. What you have now is a free-for-all so far as wages are concerned and it is a serious concern now whether clubs can afford to pay the kind of money which is being talked about.'

Manchester City manager Kevin Keegan puts it this way: 'The balance of power [between players and clubs] has shifted 180 degrees since my playing days. Players [whose contracts were up and who were negotiating a new deal] were told:

"You are getting a fiver a week – take it or leave it, and if you do not take it, we will hold your registration." They could do that, but it was wrong. Then we had Bosman, and players have been getting their own back on clubs big style.'

Of course, not all of them are in a position to do so. In the Nationwide League, for example, clubs hit by dire financial problems as a result of the collapse of ITV Digital have exploited the Bosman ruling by putting enough players on the out-of-work open-to-offers list to create a strong supply and demand situation in their favour. But it is a different matter for the players at the top end of the scale.

All of this helps explain why Southampton's Gordon Strachan suggests that his seven years as a manager have been the most difficult period ever for the individuals filling this role. Strachan, who played for Ferguson at Aberdeen and Manchester United, pointed out in his column for the *Observer* that a number of players – with more than a little help from agents – have become mercenary. 'You have to treat some of them with kid gloves,' he added. 'If you upset them, they are quite capable of downing tools. Because of their high basic salaries, being left out of the team does not hurt them.'

Strachan recalls asking Ferguson for a transfer from Aberdeen in 1982. Strachan had two years left on his contract with the club and says: 'The conversation with Fergie lasted about 30 seconds, with Fergie just saying "No", and following it up with some expletives. That was the end of the matter as far as I was concerned – I just buckled down and carried on as normal. I had no choice really. I had to play well and stay in the first team in order to be able to afford things like a good holiday each year and, of course, there was no Bosman ruling then.'

By way of an example of the increase in player power, Strachan is also fond of recalling how a player once attempted to 'blackmail' him. Strachan had a disagreement with him over a disciplinary matter and the player – whom Strachan knew was being tapped by another club – tried to get the manager to back down in the dispute with a veiled threat about the possibility of a decline in his performances. He told Strachan: 'I have been very happy here – but I can easily become unsettled.'

Others worth listening to on the subject include Alan Hansen and Eddie Gray. Both, like Strachan, are Scottish, and both, also like Strachan, can be counted among the most successful players in Britain since the war. Hansen, a key member of great Liverpool teams under the management of Bob Paisley, Joe Fagan and Kenny Dalglish, says: 'My income depended a great deal on what the club won. In my first season at Liverpool – 1977/78 – my basic salary was £7,500. The bonus for reaching the European Cup Final against Bruges that season was only £250, but the payment for winning the trophy was £6,000. Over the years, my bonuses became a smaller part of my overall income. For example, in my second season at Liverpool, my basic salary was increased to £15,000, and the bonus I received for Liverpool winning the

Championship was £6,000. But for the modern day player, the differential is so wide as to be unbelievable. Is it any wonder that a lot of managers have detected a change in players' attitudes?

'The erosion of club commitment among players can also be attributed to the influx of so many foreign players. They have raised the skill level of our football, but whether their temperaments and mentalities are generally compatible with all aspects of the traditional British team or club ethic is another matter.'

Eddie Gray, who had a similarly long playing career at the top with Leeds United (most notably in Don Revie's team of the 1960s and 1970s), and has also filled various management and coaching posts at the club, says: 'There is no doubt that it is harder to motivate players now. The money has not had much of an effect on the mentalities of genuinely great players like Roy Keane and David Beckham. They still drive themselves hard in training and matches – that is what makes them great players. But many others get into what I call the "comfort zone" and do need pushing.

'To varying degrees, players generally have always needed strong handling. Human nature being what it is, players have never been averse to looking for excuses when they have not been performing well, and taking advantage of any opportunities not to give 100 per cent. In my day, there were plenty of players who, if told to run flat out for 400 yards in training, were quite happy to limit it to 350 yards if they did not have someone pushing them.

'This is where strong managers and coaches came into their own – managers who had no compunctions about exploiting the sense of insecurity in players then. That sense of insecurity has become less pronounced and I would say that, because of the desperation of clubs to achieve success and the shortage of stars who can help them get it, some managers are too soft with players. It is easy to appreciate the trend for clubs to employ psychologists to help managers get the best out of players.

Beckham runs with the ball during the Euro 2004 qualifying match against Liechtenstein, 29 March 2003. England won 2–0. (Laurence Griffiths/Getty Images)

Alex Ferguson gives instructions from the bench during the FC Basel v Man Utd Champions League match on 26 November 2002. Man Utd won 1–3. (Ben Radford/Getty Images)

Hero to Zero. Becks is sent off by referee Kim Nielsen after lashing out at Diego Simeone during England's World Cup second round match against Argentina on 30 June 1998. England lost the match 4–3 on penalties. (Ross Kinnaird/Getty Images)

Beckham was BBC Sports Personality of the Year in 2001, the year Ferguson received a lifetime achievement award. Ellen MacArthur came second in the poll and Michael Owen third. (Warren Little/Getty Images)

The England team present Nelson Mandela with a shirt while in Durban for a friendly game against South Africa. (Touchline/Getty Images)

Sir Alex Ferguson and Willie Carson discuss form before Ferguson's horse Rock of Gibraltar ran in the 2002 St James Palace Stakes at Ascot. (Julian Herbert/Getty Images)

The new haircut. Beckham in Durban during the friendly against South Africa on 22 May 2003. England won 2–1. (Phil Cole/Getty Images)

The Beckhams at New Tokyo International Airport on their promotional tour of Japan, June 2003. (Koichi Kamoshida/Getty Images)

A Man Utd fan's farewell, Bangkok, Thailand, June 2003. (Paula Bronstein/Getty Images)

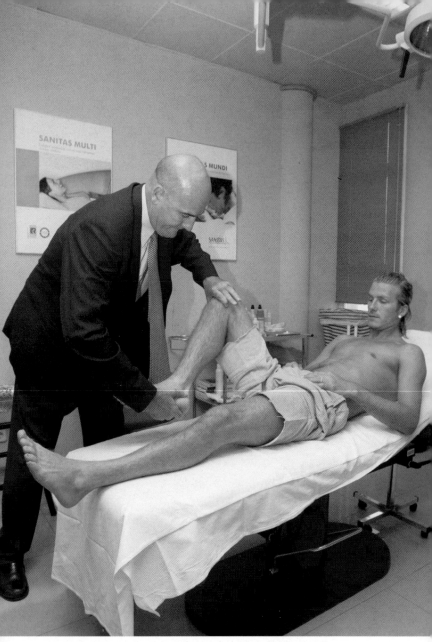

The Real Madrid medical in full view of the world's press. (Real Madrid/Getty Images)

'I am not complaining about the money I earned at Leeds, but I never made enough to make me think that I could give up working. In the Premiership, and especially the top half of it, players' salaries of around £1 million have been the norm. If a player signs a contract for that amount for four or five years, it does not take a genius to work out that, if he is careful with his spending, early retirement is not going to present major financial problems for him.

'My basic view of all this is good luck to them. Nobody can blame players for making the most of their financial opportunities. At the same time, I cannot help thinking that clubs being forced to reduce their wage bills – as has started to happen – will be a good thing for the game. It should certainly make it easier for players to keep out of that "comfort zone" and maintain their hunger for success.'

The comfort zone is not something with which any of the teams managed by Ferguson will be familiar.

It is impossible not to admire his ability to keep driving his teams to fresh heights, although even Fergie will concede that he has been helped by not having had to build those sides solely with established stars from other clubs.

It is not often that the youth system of any club produces a group of talented players good enough for first-team football at the same time. When this happens, as it did at Manchester United in the mid-1990s, a manager's chances of producing a consistently successful team over a lengthy period are significantly boosted. Through being brought up together, these players develop a strong sense of responsibility towards each other and their club. Moreover, in cases where the manager's relationship with them stretches back to the beginning of their careers – a stage in their lives when they are inclined to be particularly impressionable – there is plenty of scope for him to mould them and imbue them with the right professional habits. In that situation, he becomes more than just their football team manager – he is also something of a father-figure.

The feeling of being indebted to a manager (and thus the willingness to be subservient to him) is inevitably particularly strong when the boss gives a player his first-team chance. Eddie Gray can easily relate to Ferguson's influence on those players because his Leeds team under Don Revie was also noted for having an unusually high number of home-grown youngsters who had come through the ranks together – and Revie, too, was no shrinking violet when it came to imposing his authority on them.

Gray says: 'Don was referred to as the Leeds Godfather, and I think that was a good name for him in a lot of ways. While he was not as volatile as Alex Ferguson, he had a similarly intimidating aura. I remember Norman Hunter [one of the team's toughest characters] talking about the first and only time he was ever late for training at Leeds. Don just walked a couple of yards towards Norman, and looked at his watch. That was all he did and all he needed to do to make Norman feel bad about it.

'He was a very strong character and when he was angry about something, we were liable to be quite sensitive about doing or saying anything which might make things worse.

'He was a big man with big hands – I particularly remember the hands because when he brought his fists down on a table – something he often did when angry – the whole room seemed to reverberate.

'Suffice it to say that when he spoke, you listened. I think there was a good example during a Leeds match at Nottingham Forest, which was abandoned at half-time because of a fire in the main stand. We were listening to Don's half-time team-talk so intently that most of us were completely oblivious to the wisps of smoke coming through the dressing-room door. Gary Sprake noticed it, but when he tried to draw Bill Bremner's attention to it, Billy said: "Shut up, Gary – the boss is talking."'

For those close to the Leeds camp in those

days, it was difficult to avoid the feeling that Revie could be protective of his players to the point of possessiveness. Not surprisingly, it was a facet of his management that became increasingly difficult to maintain as they grew older and more worldly. Some of the players' wives were known to take a dim view of his control over their partners.

One incident which summed up what can happen in such player–manager relationships when footballers develop lives outside the game occurred during Leeds' trip to Italy for the European Fairs Cup Final first leg against Juventus in May 1971. Revie had decided to take the players' wives and girlfriends on the trip so they could spend some time with their partners immediately after the game; and although the match was abandoned after 51 minutes because of a waterlogged pitch, he saw no reason why the arrangement should be changed. Later that night, however, he became embroiled in a row with four players, who wanted to stay with their partners instead of having to go back to the team hotel to prepare for the rearranged game two days later. Revie won that battle, and received personal apologies not just from the players but from their wives too.

One has to suspect that the wives and girlfriends of most of the Manchester United players are even more reluctant to say or do anything that might upset Fergie. Treading with care has certainly been the watchword for their men.

Those Fergie 'Hairdrier' verbal tirades, not to mention his widely reported tendency to throw missiles around the dressing room, have always been a prominent part of his managerial approach. 'If I am displeased about a performance, I have to let the players know about it,' he has said. 'I am not one for a two- or three-day cooling-off period before I voice my feelings. That is just not my style.'

When I asked him once about the effectiveness of this approach, he replied: 'People respond to anger, don't they?' Ferguson then mentioned a player by the name of Gordon Simpson, who was his captain at the start of his managerial career at East Stirlingshire. The two men had a number of clashes, but Fergie insisted that these had a stimulating effect on Simpson's performances. Ferguson recalled one period in which Simpson was troubled by a cartilage problem. 'The cartilage would pop out during games, but every time it happened, Gordon would just grimace and push it back in.'

One criticism often levelled at Ferguson is that, in looking for the mental strength that he deems essential for success, he expects players to be cast in his mould and is not sensitive enough to the fact that different personalities and temperaments respond to different motivational methods. Ferguson himself seemed to acknowledge the point when he joined Manchester United. In his early days at Old Trafford, he told me that he found English footballers (and especially the big-name ones) very different in temperament and personality from those with whom he had been associated in Scotland. Ferguson felt that the latter were generally less sensitive, less liable to crumble if a manager got 'stuck into' them.

Fergie says he has mellowed a little with age: 'I no longer have that burning desire to change the world.' Even so, he has never believed in giving players the impression that he might be going soft. Jim McGregor, the former Manchester United physiotherapist, recalls: 'There was one match when Fergie was ranting at the players so much at half-time that I decided to go out of the dressing room and wait in the corridor. Fergie, red-faced, was the first to come out when the bell rang for the players to go back on to the field; and when he caught sight of me, he just gave a big grin and winked.'

Only in retrospect can the players on the receiving end of Fergie tirades smile about their experiences. Perhaps typical of the way they recall these outbursts is Gordon Strachan's version of a below-par performance that led to a clearly irritated Ferguson substituting him in the first half. Strachan headed straight for the bath and elected to remain in it – out of Fergie's sight – when he heard the manager come in at half-time and give the team a rollicking. 'The water was getting colder and colder,' Strachan said, 'and I kept thinking about what he would say to me if he clapped eyes on me. I was wishing I had a snorkel.'

Not surprisingly, Fergie's image as a man occasionally in need of anger-management counselling has sometimes worked against him. It is believed that some players he has wanted for his teams have turned down the chance of working with him as a result of this image. As for those who have worked with him, Eric Black, the ex-Aberdeen centre-forward, says: 'You were tested constantly whether you were good enough, could you come through it, were you mentally strong enough to go and become a player at his club. There was certainly a fear factor there, no doubt about it, and that's probably the way he wanted it.' Mark McGhee, another ex-Aberdeen striker adds: 'Every time the team was read out, I breathed a sigh of relief that my name was there. You'd played the last hundred games or so, so why wouldn't you be playing? But it was because he kept you believing that you were under pressure and your place was under threat and that you had to play well to keep it.'

Gordon Strachan adds: 'Fergie's management style has led to a number of casualties and it could be argued that some who have fallen by the wayside might well have fared better had they been handled differently. But then, when you look at the number of players who have blossomed under his management, and his record, who can say that his way of doing things isn't right?'

Beckham certainly responded to Fergie's form of management, as he acknowledged when publicly drawing attention to the manager's part in his development as a top player just after his move to Real Madrid. However, it was only to be expected that Fergie's control over Beckham would eventually become weaker than it is over the other 'Fergie Fledgelings'.

None of them has a life outside professional football like Beckham's. And how many other players' wives can be compared to Posh Spice?

Chapter Four

The Posh Effect

If any event can be described as the turning point in the relationship between Ferguson and Beckham, it is what happened off the field on 15 March 1997, the day Manchester United beat Sheffield Wednesday 2–0 in an Old Trafford league match. Among the female members of the crowd whose attention was drawn mainly to Beckham was Victoria Adams.

She was not a football fan, but had agreed to accompany fellow Spice Girl Mel C to the game. Afterwards Posh Spice and Beckham were introduced, a meeting largely prompted by her. That evening they went out for a meal with Mel C and United's Ryan Giggs.

For Beckham and Victoria the attraction was mutual. Within a matter of weeks they were besotted with each other, and from that point Beckham had another hugely powerful influence in his life, other than Alex Ferguson.

From the day the couple met Fergie's control over Becks started to weaken. At the outset of the Becks–Posh romance, Fergie must have found it irksome enough to have a love-sick youngster on his hands, who seemed to feel that if he couldn't see the object of his desire every day – or at least spend hours talking to her on the phone – he might suffer nose-bleeds. For Posh, too, it was a question of absence making the heart grow fonder. She was as committed to keeping in touch as he was. But because she had no knowledge of the requirements of his job – the culture of professional football – she didn't always pick the right moments.

The former United forward Brian McClair has revealed that Victoria, much to Beckham's embarrassment, once called him on his mobile while Ferguson was delivering a pre-match team-talk. To his credit, Fergie didn't bat an eyelid. Like a teacher tired of raising his voice to get the attention of a distracted pupil, he just strode across to Beckham, picked up the mobile and dropped it in a bin.

But what Fergie perceived as his Beckham problems were about to get worse. Beckham was becoming more than just a top professional footballer. He was going down a lifestyle road that some experts interpreted as a threat to his development as a player and therefore to the group dynamics of the team.

Ferguson is hardly alone in believing that managers have a duty to instil their beliefs and professional habits into their young players. This often means protecting players from the distractions and temptations that represent career banana-skins for them outside their clubs – in a sense, protecting impressionable young men from themselves. Not long after breaking into Fergie's Aberdeen first team as a teenager, midfielder Neale Cooper, who had been living with his parents, bought a flat for himself in the city. But he had to get rid of it and move back with his mother and father when Fergie found out: 'He just said to me: "You are too young to be living on your own." That was it.'

At Manchester United Ferguson was particularly determined to protect Ryan Giggs. The brilliant Welsh winger, who had been persuaded by Fergie to switch his allegiance from Manchester City to United when he was 14, is arguably the most talented of all the players the manager has brought through the Old Trafford ranks. Nicknamed the 'Welsh Wizard', he was only 18 when he established himself in the team, but it was some time before Fergie – conscious of what too much money and fame could do to a player – allowed him to make his own decisions concerning endorsement deals, sponsorship offers and requests for media interviews.

The most recent example of a manager striving to keep a player's feet firmly on the ground concerns Everton's David Moyes, and his precocious 17-year-old striker, Wayne

Rooney. At various times during the 2002/03 season 'Beckham-mania' was replaced by 'Rooney-mania'. In the opening months of the season, Rooney was not very well known outside Merseyside. But all that changed in October 2002 when the teenager, five days before his 17th birthday, was brought on as a substitute (his usual role) at home against Arsenal. It was only his 10th first-team appearance but with the highlights of the match shown on ITV that night, Rooney made it one to remember for millions by producing a superb last-minute lob over keeper David Seaman from 35 yards to give Everton a 2–1 win.

Since then, Rooney, or 'Roonaldo' as the tabloids have tagged him, has been hailed as the future saviour of English football. But the publicity bandwagon has set off loud alarms in the ears of those responsible for his football development at Everton. As a result of that goal, the centre-point of a performance in which Rooney had run the Arsenal defence ragged, Moyes inevitably came under intense pressure to make him a more integral part of his team.

It was the same story with England manager Sven-Goran Eriksson, who had to contend with an even more concerted campaign to give Rooney his chance at senior international level. In February 2003, the Rooney-hype reached another level when Eriksson brought him on as substitute in the 2–0 defeat by Australia, making him the youngest-ever England player (at 17 years and 111 days). By the end of the season, Rooney had taken part in four further England matches – including European Championship qualifying ties against Liechtenstein, Turkey and Slovenia – and picked up the BBC TV Young Sports Personality of the Year award.

But through all of this, the sound of David Moyes's protests could be heard in the background. In trying to prevent Rooney getting carried away by his fame, or inviting unreasonable expectations of his capabilities, Moyes was less than enthusiastic about those England call-ups. Moyes and Eriksson were involved in one of the biggest disputes of the season over Rooney's selection for the squad for the match against South Africa in Durban in May 2003 (a row that was resolved by Everton convincing the FA that Rooney could not go on the trip because of injury). Moyes put it this way: 'I think he [Rooney] needs to be developed. We are trying to bring him on in the correct manner. Too many young players are raved about for a year and supposed to be the best thing since sliced bread, and then they drop away. We have been telling people we are trying to nurture him and not give him too much too soon. His ability's not questioned but he's not ready to do it week in, week out. You have to remember that only seven months ago, he was sitting behind a school desk. Let's put it in perspective.'

On the face of it, the general record of British managers in helping talented footballers to realise their potential is not very impressive. As Moyes indicated, the game has been littered with agonising cases of stars who seemed to have it all but then left their admirers with a deep sense of disappointment at their apparent underachievement. Generally, the players who have had the most successful careers have been those with comparatively less ability – those for whom standing out on a football field has been more difficult and who thus have had no option but to work hard and apply themselves properly.

Of all the examples in the first category, the one who provokes the most discussion is George Best. The rise and fall of his career is particularly poignant to followers of Manchester United because Best, of course, is acknowledged as the greatest player in the club's history. The dazzling winger, who joined the club at 15 and made his debut at 17 in September 1963, appeared in a total of 361 first-team matches in 10 years there and scored 137 goals. He steered United to two Championship triumphs and victory in the European Cup.

In the 1964/65 European Cup, he and United were the talk of football all over the world as a result of a mind-boggling 5–1 second-leg

quarter-final trouncing of Benfica in Lisbon –
the first time that the Portuguese giants had lost
a European tie at home. With United holding
only a one-goal lead from the first leg, manager
Matt Busby told his team to 'keep it tight' for
the first 15 minutes. But as Busby observed later,
when drily suggesting that the player had
'probably not been listening to me', Best had
other ideas. He destroyed Benfica's morale in the
opening 12 minutes by scoring twice.

In May 1968, when Best's irrepressible skills
again undermined Benfica in the European Cup
Final at Wembley, the nationwide outpouring of
admiration and affection for him was as
powerful as it was for David Beckham when he
put England through to the 2002 World Cup
Finals with that dramatic goal against Greece.

Although he was viewed as arguably the
greatest footballer of all time for any British
club, many people have been left with the feeling
that Best still did not achieve all that he could
have done. He was 27 when he left United – an
age when he would have been expected to be at

his peak – and that marked the end of his status as a top-flight player.

It is a story that has come to the fore again recently, not just through Best's struggle to overcome his life-threatening drink problems but also because of the status Beckham has gained.

Comparisons are inevitable. In many ways, Best was the David Beckham of his day. He was the first player truly to transcend the traditional football stereotype and become a powerful cultural symbol of his time. It is only since Beckham's arrival on the English football stage that the void left by Best has been filled.

Best's rise to prominence in the 1960s coincided with the increase in television coverage of the game. (It was in 1964 that the BBC started its *Match of the Day* programme.) It also coincided with the explosion of pop culture. The rebellious, individualistic elements in his style of play seemed to fit the mood of the era perfectly. The Beatles, coming to the fore at the same time as Best did at Old Trafford, provided the most potent manifestation of that explosion; and because Best himself looked as though he wouldn't be out of place on stage with them, he became known as 'The Fifth Beatle'.

Like Beckham, he seemed very different as a person from a lot of other young professional footballers. Eamonn Dunphy, who started his own playing career at Manchester United at the same time as Best, and is now one of the most outspoken and perceptive commentators on the game, recalled that he was 'shy and watchful of manner'. He added: 'There was something different about Best from the beginning. He wasn't as coarse as the rest of us players. He did not swear or talk dirty about girls. He used shampoo instead of soap in his hair. He was a popular lad but never a Lad in the true dressing-room sense of that word.'

Another similarity between Best and Beckham is that Best generated a big income outside football. He did some modelling, notably for the Great Universal Stores catalogue, and his list of endorsement contracts for non-football-related products included appearances in TV advertising campaigns for Irish sausages, Spanish oranges and the Egg Marketing Board. At his peak, he was receiving so many fan letters – 10,000 a week – that he needed a full-time staff of three to deal with them. He was mobbed everywhere he went. His collection of expensive clothes and cars reflected the fact that he had money to burn, and he was not short of girlfriends. The combination of his fame, his dark good looks and his Irish charm attracted glamorous females galore.

But Best had a wayward streak. His lack of discipline, especially with regard to his struggle to resist the temptations of birds and booze, caught up with him. To his credit Best himself has readily admitted that a lot of his problems were self-inflicted. He has also expressed some regret that nobody at Manchester United was able to control him.

In those days, the media coverage of football was nowhere near as intensive – and intrusive – as it is today, so Best was able to get away with more than today's stars can. Matt Busby did take action against him occasionally – in addition to lecturing him about his conduct outside the club, Busby dropped him from the first team and imposed club fines on him. Even so, Best suggests that Busby could and should have been harder on him. According to Best, Busby was sensitive about the effect of disciplinary action against the player on United's public image.

Best has also said that Busby's attitude towards him was influenced by his footballing ability. 'Poor old Matt was caught between the pit and the pendulum,' Best said. 'He wanted to get me to toe the line, but he also knew that I was his greatest asset, who could be his leading player for another 15 years. I was also the one who could deliver his European dream so he never really came down on me like a ton of bricks. The normal laws of the club did not seem to apply to me.'

By the time Busby stepped down as manager and became general manager, in the summer of

1969, Best's wayward streak was sufficiently ingrained to make him a difficult man for anyone to control. This hardly made life easier for Busby's successors, who had more than enough headaches in other departments in dealing with a United team in decline.

Busby's immediate successor was Wilf McGuinness, a former United player, who was only 31 when he was promoted from the coaching staff at Old Trafford to take charge of the first team. McGuinness only lasted 18 months in the job before being demoted to the position of reserve-team coach. Many observers have assumed that the stress he experienced in that short period contributed to the fact that all his hair fell out in a matter of weeks.

Of course, if any footballer seems not to need strict managerial control, it is David Beckham. He appears to have no trace of a self-destructive streak. No footballer can work harder in training and matches than Beckham. Disarmingly modest and willing to laugh at himself, he does not smoke and he is the very last player who could be expected to get into drugs or gambling. And though he can be hot-headed during matches, his conduct outside football appears exemplary. Happily married, and with two children he clearly dotes on, he is very much the contented family man.

The irony of Ferguson's concern that Beckham was allowing other aspects of his life to detract from his commitment to Manchester United and football is that similar fears were reported to have been expressed about the manager's own commitment by some members of the United board. It was claimed that some at Old Trafford were worried Ferguson's involvement in horse-racing as an owner and the writing of his autobiography (the first massive draft of which he penned himself) might divert his full attention away from the club.

However, the non-football distractions for Ferguson can hardly be compared to Beckham's. The biggest is the so-called celebrity circus in which Beckham has become embroiled – the extraordinary media attention he attracts, his big endorsement and advertising deals, and the involvement he and Victoria have in the elite fashion and entertainment social scene. Posh and Becks are arguably the most photographed and talked-about couple in the world, and there is little evidence to suggest that they aren't happy to keep it that way.

For all the glitter and glamour in Beckham's life, not all professional football figures would want to be in his shoes. This particularly applies to the men who earned their football livings at a time when the celebrity culture in England was less pronounced than it is today and the game was less media-driven. The first on that list is Ferguson.

Just before the 1998 World Cup Finals in France, Ferguson travelled with Posh and Becks on a flight from Nice to London's Heathrow. The media pressure the couple experienced – with newspaper photographers dogging their every step – clearly went beyond anything Fergie had ever seen in his career. 'I cannot imagine ever wanting to give even a minute of my life to the sort of nonsense that surrounded David that day,' Ferguson has said.

Strange as it might seem, one former star who would also have hated it is Alan Hansen. During his Liverpool career from 1977 to 1991, Hansen collected as many as 17 major competition winners' medals. Yet he admits that he suffered with nerves before almost every game, and afterwards he was among the first players to leave the ground and return to the privacy of his family life. He was notoriously reticent when it came to media interviews. 'I would usually find a way to avoid them,' he once told me. 'I am a person whose life needs to be as basic and straightforward as possible.' He also admitted that when he came into contact with Beckham, Michael Owen and Alan Shearer for his television documentary on the lifestyles of modern players (*Football Millionaires*), his main reaction to their 'goldfish bowl' existence was that they should be 'pitied rather than envied'. Hansen recalled the way in which Adidas publicly launched their association with

Beckham – a glitzy presentation in which he was unveiled in a cloud of dry ice. 'He did look a bit self-conscious,' Hansen says. 'But had it been me, I would have been hiding in the toilet.'

Beckham's apparent self-consciousness could have been misleading. Far from fighting shy of the limelight, he seems to relish it. Even the most disturbing aspects of the fame he and Posh have gained – such as the personal security threats to the Beckhams as a family and to their son Brooklyn in particular – don't seem to have adversely affected his football performances.

For that reason alone, many people felt Ferguson was being churlish in expressing concern about the Beckham 'circus'. But, in the light of the argument that a top footballer's life needs to become narrower as he gets older – that he needs to be more focused than ever on his career in the game in order to keep up his standards – Fergie's stance was understandable.

There has also been a feeling that the distraction of 'Beckham-mania' could rebound on the player's teams. Beckham's transfer to

Real Madrid, when all United's fixtures had been completed, coincided with the Spanish club's build-up to their last league match of the season – a match they needed to win to clinch the La Liga title. Real's players were clearly taken aback by the media frenzy surrounding Beckham's move – so much so that Beckham, conscious of the effect this might have on their performance, felt it necessary to make a public apology to them.

On their summer tour of the United States, Manchester United seemed considerably more relaxed without Beckham than they would have been with him. For example, they did not need to have Fort Knox-type security at their hotels. United's chief executive Peter Kenyon pointed out: 'One thing his absence has done is to take the heat off the rest of the squad. It has been so much more relaxed. They have been able to walk the streets without lots of people being around for the wrong reasons.'

Beckham does not conduct himself like an A-list celebrity either inside the dressing room or on the field. But at Manchester United, the attention on him made it difficult to escape the impression of an XI comprising Beckham and ten others. It was inevitable that, subconsciously at least, Beckham would become a man apart there.

The combined personal fortune of Mr and Mrs Beckham has been estimated at more than £60 million, with Beckham reckoned to have the financial edge in the relationship on the £38 million mark. At Manchester United, Beckham earned £90,000 a week (£20,000 of which covered his image rights) and was reported to be raking in another £10–£15 million a year from personal sponsorship deals. In addition to their lavish multi-million pound properties, the couple's awesome financial power can also be seen in their garages. At the last count, Beckham owned three Mercedes (including an armoured model), two Ferraris, a Bentley and a Lincoln Navigator – a collection worth some £800,000. Such is Beckham's celebrity status that he no longer needs to be

...sful as a footballer for his wealth and ...e to be maintained.

At United, the difference between Beckham and the rest was further illustrated by the fact that, while the other players lived within easy travelling distance of the club's training ground, he – partly, it was reported, because of Victoria's reluctance to live in Cheshire – chose to make his main family home on the outskirts of London. 'Beckingham Palace' is in Sawbridgeworth, Hertfordshire.

Ferguson has always been a great admirer of Beckham's inner strength. As he has said: 'Nobody should ever underestimate David Beckham.' But Fergie has also been in the game long enough to know how easily money and fame can affect a player's hunger for success. Beckham himself, referring to the changes in his life just before his second son Romeo was born, was quoted as saying: 'Football is not the only thing in my life any more. Things that were important before just do not seem as important now that I have Brooklyn and Victoria.'

Many of the Manchester United followers who were upset by the Fergie–Beckham rift, and what it led to, might well consider that Victoria has a lot to answer for. She has a more forceful personality than Beckham, and there is little doubt that, though he is far from being the under-the-thumb husband that some have made him out to be, she has a big influence on him. There is little doubt, either, that the conflict between Ferguson and Beckham has led to just as much friction – if not more – between Ferguson and Posh. A source reportedly close to Posh and Becks was once quoted as saying: 'Victoria's comments have got David into trouble [with Ferguson] and David has had to ask her to be more discreet. Posh often has quite a bit to say, and is extremely protective over David. That can be a volatile combination.' That Ferguson could never hope for a dinner invitation from Victoria was emphasised by her father Tony in an interview on LBC radio in May 2003. Asked by LBC presenter Nick Ferrari what his daughter thought about Ferguson, Adams paused before replying and said: 'Umm – can I say the famous "no comment"?'

The nickname 'Posh' stems from Victoria's middle-class upbringing. Tony Adams had a successful electrical wholesale business, and the family's social status meant that Victoria had no problems standing out from the crowd when she was growing up. After all, the house she lived in had a swimming pool, and her father took her to school each day in his Rolls-Royce.

Like Beckham, Victoria is a difficult person to truly dislike. Stunningly feminine and with a mischievous sense of humour, she comes over well in TV interviews. But her obvious charm and warmth are underpinned by an impression that she is a pushy lady who likes nothing better than to be the centre of attention. Some tabloids have not been very kind to Victoria Beckham. One writer, for example, has described her as being 'addicted' to fame.

If that really is the case, it does not seem to have affected Beckham's career to date.

Chapter Five

Hero to Zero to Hero

It is likely that David Beckham would still be a Manchester United player if Alex Ferguson had followed through with his intention of retiring as a manager at the end of the 2001/02 season.

Not only that, Beckham's position at Old Trafford would probably have become more powerful than ever in Fergie's absence. He would have had a good chance of being appointed team captain, the position he fills in the England set-up but which was denied him on a permanent basis at Old Trafford, and he would have had an even better chance of getting the central midfield role he wanted.

Just as in the England team, he would probably also have had a manager who didn't shout and scream at him, because the man reckoned to have the best chance of succeeding Fergie at Old Trafford was Sven-Goran Eriksson.

Fergie changed his mind about stepping down in February 2002 after his family convinced him that he still had much to offer in the job and would badly miss his close involvement in the game, but he was less than discreet about his proposed successor. He suggested – in an interview with Robert Crampton in *The Times* magazine – that Eriksson and the United board had actually reached a provisional agreement for the Swede to take over.

'I think they'd done the deal all right,' Fergie said. 'I do not know for certain, but I am sure it was Eriksson, you know?' Crampton asked if Eriksson had signed a contract. 'No, no, no,' Ferguson replied. 'I think they'd shaken hands. They could not put anything on paper because he was still England manager.'

But the most intriguing part of the interview

was Fergie's view of Eriksson. His comments included putting on a Swedish accent and mimicking one of Eriksson's typically bland post-match comments about his team. Referring to Eriksson's personality, Fergie said: 'I think Sven Eriksson would have been a nice easy choice for them [the United board] in terms of nothing really happens, does it? He doesna change anything. He sails along, nobody falls out with him. Carlos Queiroz [Fergie's assistant at United then] knows him because he [Eriksson] was with Benfica and Carlos is from Lisbon [the city in which the club are based]. Carlos says that what he did well was he never fell out with anyone, [he was] best pal with the president [of the club], the press liked him . . .'

Fergie even suggested that some of Eriksson's decisions – and notably his appointment of Beckham as England captain – had been partly influenced by the media. Whatever the truth of that, Ferguson hardly needed to say that he and Eriksson are as different as people and managers as it is possible for any two men to be. Nobody would ever dream of suggesting that Fergie is too dispassionate to truly lift his teams, as has been the case with Eriksson.

When Eriksson became England's first foreign national team coach in January 2001, his low-key, almost professorial approach – his ability to distance himself from the hysteria that often surrounds the England team – seemed a big plus-point. But before long, it was reckoned to be his – and England's – major flaw.

It was for this reason that Eriksson took much of the blame for England's 2–1 defeat by Brazil in the 2002 World Cup quarter-final. Even after taking into account the renowned skills of the team they were playing, England seemed strangely subdued. They held their own for much of the first half in which Michael Owen's early opening goal was cancelled out by Rivaldo, but they didn't appear to derive much confidence from this. Early in the second half, that extraordinary cross-cum-shot from Ronaldinho, which went over David Seaman and into the net, didn't help matters. But when England were then handed a potential lifeline as Ronaldinho was sent off, their response was somewhat muted.

Though Eriksson attributed it to his players' tiredness, this interpretation was offset by the feeling that he might not have done enough at half-time to wake them up. Indeed, some time afterwards, an England defender was quoted as saying: 'Instead of Winston Churchill, we got Iain Duncan Smith.'

Eriksson has said: 'I am too old to change my character. What would be the point anyway? If anyone can guarantee me that we would have done better in the second half if I'd spent half-time shouting, then I will listen to them. But I think it is old fashioned.'

Even Arsene Wenger, who appears to be in the same studious mould as Eriksson, has been known to lose it occasionally. In the debate about Eriksson's management style, he has said: 'To survive in the English job, you need passion. It is not too difficult to lose it. The bigger the animal inside, the more you have to keep it in control, and there is a big animal in there [in himself]. You learn to control your emotions most of the time, but sometimes you have a gut reaction.' The quote appeared in a column by the *Daily Telegraph*'s football correspondent, Henry Winter. He summed it up perfectly when he observed: 'There is not enough ice in Ferguson's veins and too much ice in Eriksson's.'

Though Eriksson's approach would have taken Beckham and the other long-serving United players from one extreme to the other, that is precisely why Mr Ice Man might have been good for them.

When managers talk about their sell-by dates at clubs, they are usually referring to the problems of continuing to find new ways to have an impact on their players. There is little doubt that Fergie has done exceptionally well to maintain control and influence over such a long period. Even so, after listening to his voice for 10 years or so, Beckham and Co.

would surely have found the quieter Eriksson a refreshing change.

The other advantage for Beckham if Eriksson had replaced Fergie at Old Trafford, would have been the manager's respect and admiration for him. While Fergie seemed to be having increasingly mixed feelings about Beckham's importance to United – especially in the light of that Beckham 'circus' – Eriksson has never appeared less than 100 per cent happy with him. Beckham, who has made the vast majority of his 60 England appearances under Eriksson, indicated how much this has helped him when drawing attention to Eriksson's 'building up' of his players before matches.

In some ways, Eriksson's regard for Beckham, and his decision to make him his England captain, stem from what he has learned during his close association with the eminent Norwegian sports psychologist, Professor Willi Railo. According to Railo, Eriksson's success has been built on the principle of being able to find a group of what he describes as 'cultural architects' or 'positive energy sources'. Not long after Eriksson became England boss, Railo explained that 'cultural architects' are leaders. 'They want to take the group forward. The other group are cultural prisoners, who are negative, who tell you why something can't be done rather than how it could be done.' Railo said that Eriksson had three 'cultural leaders' at Lazio (when the coach steered the club to their first Italian Championship win for 26 years) and that he only needed that number to transform the fortunes of the England team. 'I believe Sven knows who they are already,' said Railo, but he was reticent about naming all of them publicly. But, on the premise of stating what he felt was the obvious, he was willing to give the first name on that select list – David Beckham.

'I did not fully realise what a good player he is until I started working with him,' Eriksson once said. Indeed, whenever there has been an opportunity for Eriksson to sing the player's praises publicly, he has taken it. On another occasion, after Beckham's performance in

England's 4–0 win over Mexico at Derby's Pride Park in May 2001 – encapsulated by what Eriksson described as the 'beautiful' Beckham long-range pass to Steven Gerrard which led to the second goal – Eriksson enthused: 'If you talk about our captain, it is difficult to find a better passer of the ball in the world today, certainly in Europe. I had two excellent passers at Lazio in Juan Sebastian Veron [later to become Beckham's teammate at Old Trafford] and Sinisa Mihajlovic. It is difficult to compare, but if Beckham is not better than them, he is certainly on the same level.'

Eriksson's praise for Beckham was even more fulsome, of course, on 6 October 2001, when his skipper was the inspiration for the crucial 2–2 draw against Greece that put England through to the 2002 World Cup Finals. 'I knew of Beckham before I came here,' Eriksson said. 'But I was surprised. He is much quicker than I thought, he runs much more than I thought. When you follow him from outside, from another country, you read a lot of him in newspapers, his wife and so on, and you don't know him as a person. He is a big professional, a big captain.

'Beckham played one of the best games I have ever seen him play,' he added. 'He ran all over the pitch and was a big captain for England. He did everything today to try and push the team and win the game. I am happy for him.'

Whether Ferguson felt exactly the same way is open to doubt. 'Mixed feelings' is probably the best way to describe his reaction.

It is very much a compliment to Fergie and United that Beckham and his old Trafford colleagues, including Phil and Gary Neville, Paul Scholes and Nicky Butt, have become such an integral part of the England squad. Moreover, the personal satisfaction Fergie will have derived from this is bound to have been strengthened by the ways in which United have benefited from the players' international success. As at all clubs with national players, their inclusion in the England team has helped raise United's profile and also the players' transfer-market value.

However, on the other side of the coin are the vast amounts of money at stake for the top clubs in their own football environment, and their fears that the mental and physical well-being of their stars might be undermined by too many matches and too much travelling.

There has always been a club v country conflict in British football, and with clubs investing so much of their cash in players, it has probably never been as serious as it is today. For Manchester United and their European counterparts, the general standard of play and the level of public interest in international club football have become considerably higher as a result of the ever-growing cosmopolitan nature of the teams and the development of the European Cup into the European Champions League. In contrast, the general standard of play and the level of public interest in many of the matches played by national teams have become correspondingly lower.

As a result of the political upheavals in Eastern Europe, the number of national teams –

and, of course, national team matches – has increased to the extent that, even in competitions such as the World Cup and European Championship (in the preliminary stages at least), some games tend to be uninspiring.

It could be argued that the overall standard of football in Premiership teams is higher than that in a number of national sides. This particularly applies to the Premiership giants like Manchester United, Arsenal, Liverpool and Chelsea. In view of the high number of great players from other countries in club line-ups, it is not unreasonable to suggest that had one of those teams been able to compete in the World Cup Finals in Korea and Japan, they would have had a good chance of winning the competition.

Another reason why clubs feel justified in putting their interests above the interests of national teams is that they get no financial compensation for a national federation's use of their players. In a recent BBC TV programme on the subject, *Football: Club or Country?*, it was pointed out that if Beckham (still a United player then) were to be involved in all nine scheduled England matches in 2003 (six competitive games and three friendlies), the amount of time he would be away from the club would amount to something like 45 days. To put it another way, United would have been paying him more than £500,000 to play for England. The point was further underlined by the similar example of Arsenal's most influential player, their French international midfielder Patrick Vieira.

In the light of the numerous headaches associated with releasing players for international duty, the attitude of Ferguson – and all the other managers who would like nothing better than to be able to keep their stars permanently under their control – is understandable.

Fergie's stance has not brought him many admirers, though. After all, he was a national team manager once. Having been Jock Stein's right-hand man in the Scotland set-up for the qualifying rounds of the 1986 World Cup, he took charge of the squad – as a result of Stein's death during the Scots' last preliminary tie against Wales – for the finals in Mexico. Another reason why he is inclined to stand out among the Premiership bosses who are less than enamoured of releasing players for national squad service is that, with the possible exception of Gerard Houllier who has Steven Gerrard and Michael Owen at Liverpool, Fergie has had England's most important players.

Fergie's image among England supporters was hardly enhanced when Paul Scholes missed the friendly against Portugal in September 2002. The Saturday before Eriksson announced his squad for the game, Scholes missed United's match at Sunderland because of an ankle injury. The following Monday, after United had confirmed that Scholes was still suffering from the injury, Eriksson crossed him off his list. The next day, however, Eriksson attended United's home match against Middlesbrough – and the starting line-up included Scholes. He played for 79 minutes.

Not being in any position to stage an all-out war against managers like Ferguson, Eriksson has always been diplomatic about the United boss's cooperation limits. But Eriksson's mother Ulla appeared to hit out on his behalf when she allegedly claimed that Ferguson was a 'threat' to her son. In a Swedish newspaper interview (which an embarrassed Eriksson insisted to Fergie had never taken place) she was quoted as saying: 'Alex Ferguson is a threat to my son. Sven told me during a phone conversation that it is pointless having national team games in April or May [the most crucial period of the season for clubs chasing honours] because Ferguson, in one way or another, makes sure his stars are not fit.'

When it comes to managers putting pressure on players not to turn out for their country, some inevitably resist more than others. Beckham could certainly be expected to be unhappy about being asked to choose between club and country. The England captaincy, which was initially handed to him by Peter Taylor when Taylor was caretaker manager for one match (against Italy) following the sacking of Glenn Hoddle, but which was taken away from him by Hoddle's successor, Kevin Keegan, is a responsibility that means a great deal to him.

Apart from anything else, the position has made it easier for Beckham to gain credibility as a world-class player. This has been important to him because, while he doesn't appear to have a big ego, he does – like most outstanding footballers – need and want to be able to demonstrate his full capabilities. Beckham was once asked whether he felt that, deep down, he was a bit of a 'showman'. 'Probably,' he acknowledged. As England captain, Beckham's ability has had maximum exposure. This, perhaps, goes a long way towards explaining the theory that he plays even better for Eriksson than he did for Ferguson.

On the basis of making sure that a player's efforts on behalf of the national team do not rebound against his club side, Ferguson clearly had mixed feelings about the energy Beckham expended against Greece, and the incredible nationwide applause he was given. While the whole country was busy elevating Beckham to the status of a king, Fergie's reaction to his performance was underwhelming.

Referring to United's European Champions League clash with another Greek team, Olympiakos, in Athens the following week, Fergie said: 'I think captaining England has inspired the lad – there's no question about that. But the media coverage [of Beckham's display against Greece] has gone over the top as usual. We have got to pick up the pieces of that. I have to pick a team and bring my players back to earth.'

On the eve of the game, Ferguson even indicated that he might be forced to give Beckham a rest. While admitting that Beckham himself did not feel he needed one, Ferguson said: 'I think his efforts against Greece might have an adverse effect, so I will probably put him on the bench.' As it turned out, Beckham did get a place in United's starting line-up, and, as if to hit back at Fergie's fears about the work he had carried out on England's behalf, he scored the first goal (after 66 minutes) in a 2–0 United victory.

Ferguson's attempts to establish a greater sense of perspective on Beckham's England achievements were seen again when the player's participation in the World Cup Finals was thrown into jeopardy by injury. (He fractured a bone in his left foot during the European Champions League semi-final against Deportivo La Coruna in April 2002.) Unlike most of England, Ferguson's reaction to the possibility that Beckham would not be part of the England squad in Korea and Japan was disconcertingly philosophical.

'It's a shame,' Fergie said. 'But he is a young lad and there will be other World Cups for him.' To observers of a cynical bent, this was Fergie-type shorthand for: 'What a good thing this will be for Manchester United. Without the strain of a World Cup, he will be full of beans for us next season.'

However, although Ferguson's reaction to Beckham's great England moments might not always have been as enthusiastic as one might have expected, even Beckham would be loath to hold this against the manager. The fact is that Fergie was there for Beckham when he needed him most. Beckham's England career, while providing him with his most memorable high-spots, also brought him the lowest point of his career. When that came along, nobody gave him greater support and encouragement than Fergie.

A less helpful central figure in that dark side of the Beckham story was the then England manager, Glenn Hoddle, ironically one of Beckham's favourite non-Manchester United players as a boy.

Hoddle's appointment in 1996 at the age of 39 gave him the distinction of being the youngest-ever England manager. As a Tottenham and England player, he had been one of the most skilful midfielders in the game, and he had done well as a manager at club level with Swindon and Chelsea. But Hoddle's spell at the helm of the England team was punctuated by observations from outsiders that he was arrogant and stubborn.

As far as his relationship with Beckham was concerned, it became clear that Hoddle – who still looked the part of a top-notch footballer, not least in training – seemed to present himself as the ideal example for Beckham to follow.

One early Hoddle misgiving about Beckham concerned the player's petulance on the field. After Beckham's two bookings in the Le Tornoi World Cup rehearsal tournament in France in the summer of 1997, Hoddle said: 'The signs of a disciplinary problem are there with David and we need to stamp down on them pretty early. He gets carried away with things he should not be carried away with.'

That assessment was fair enough – Beckham has admitted himself that he could be 'hot-headed' in those days. But there were some strong mitigating circumstances, notably the fact that Beckham was subjected to baiting from the crowd because of his glamorous image and relationship with Posh Spice. Hoddle showed little understanding of this. In urging Beckham to show the same self-control that he felt he had himself displayed as a player, Hoddle overlooked two factors. The first was that the amount of stick Hoddle experienced from spectators was nothing compared to the abuse that Beckham had to deal with. The second was that his own disciplinary record was not unblemished (he was sent off twice).

But the most controversial episode in the relationship between Hoddle and Beckham took place in the 1998 World Cup Finals in France, when Beckham, having played in all England's qualifying games, was left out of the starting line-up for their opening two group matches.

After the first match against Tunisia, which England won 2–0, Beckham – strangely, one of the players put forward for media interviews even though he had played no part in the game – found it impossible to hide his disappointment. 'My stomach was turning over so many times [when Hoddle announced the team] it was unbelievable,' he said.

It seemed that the reasons for his exclusion had not been fully explained to him. But after the second match, a 2–1 defeat by Romania in which Beckham had come on as a substitute for Paul Ince and had done well, Hoddle elected to elaborate on his decision. Echoing the doubts that Ferguson has expressed about Beckham, he said: 'I don't think he's been focused coming into this tournament. At the end of the season, he has not been focused. Perhaps his club should have looked at that earlier, but he hasn't been focused and he has just been a bit vague.'

'We have had a chat,' Hoddle added, 'and he certainly looks more focused now.' Indeed, Beckham was back in the fold for England's last group match against Colombia and scored the second goal in a 2–0 win with one of those magnificent free kicks.

Then came the match against Argentina when Beckham's worst nightmare was played out in front of a TV audience of around 30 million. He was sent off after 47 minutes with the score at 2–2 and England looking a good bet to win.

Nobody, least of all Beckham, could dispute that the action which reduced England to 10 men – a retaliatory flick of his leg at Diego Simeone, right in front of the referee, after the Argentinian midfielder had been penalised for a foul on him – was irresponsible in the extreme. Even then, as if to emphasise what they could have achieved with Beckham on the field, England continued to make Argentina sweat. No doubt motivated to some degree by the fact that the wily Simeone had made a meal of the incident, England's efforts to get themselves and Beckham out of the hole he had dug for them were remarkable. In preventing Argentina from capitalising on their numerical advantage over the remaining 31 minutes of normal time and then the 30 minutes of extra time, they fought one of the most remarkable uphill football battles of all time.

But their dreams of a place in the last eight were cruelly destroyed in the penalty shoot-out. Paul Ince and David Batty both missed. This presented another traumatic twist for Beckham because he, rather than Ince or Batty, would have been among the five England penalty-takers had he not been red-carded. Ince and Batty, and all the others who had frustrated Argentina, were acclaimed as heroes. Beckham, though, became the most despised figure in England – the target for the sort of media and public abuse usually reserved for much more serious acts in society.

For Beckham the reaction of the English newspapers was bad enough. The following day the *Mirror*'s front-page headline read: 'Ten Heroic Lions. One Stupid Boy'. The *Daily Star* devoted its front page to the comment: 'Sorry lads, no tits on page three, only Beckham'. Even the broadsheets joined in the Beckham-castigation game. The *Daily Telegraph*, for example, posed the question: 'Is Beckham what is wrong with this country?' It then described him as a 'Gaultier-saronged, Posh-Spiced, Cooled-Britannia, look-at-me, loads-of-money, sex-and-shopping, fame-schooled, daytime-TV, over-coiffed twerp'. It mattered not a jot that Beckham, devastated by his misdemeanour according to his England teammates, made a public apology for his behaviour – nor that they and Hoddle (not to mention the Bible Society and the Archbishop of Canterbury) made pleas for him to be forgiven. The English public was determined to increase his misery.

Manchester United, concerned about the prospect of violence against Beckham by opposing fans, arranged for him to have a personal bodyguard – the former SAS soldier Ned Kelly, who ran the club's private security firm and who was also Eric Cantona's minder when the Frenchman had serious unpopularity problems. There were also fears that the hostility towards Beckham would reach the stage where the only option for the player and United would be for him to move abroad.

An unnamed 'member of the Beckham family' was quoted as saying: 'David is heartbroken over what happened. He is trying to get away from the pressure at the moment [he and Posh went to New York soon after the Argentina game] but he will soon be back in training with United and he feels that this is when the problems will begin. David has told us that he will stay in England for the first two months of the season to see what sort of reaction he gets. If it is too bad, he will ask for a move abroad.' Some reports indicated that United had even offered Beckham counselling.

After the Argentina match, though, Beckham was helped by his own strength of character – few players would have been able to handle what he had to contend with – and his Manchester United colleagues. The part Ferguson and Beckham's United teammates played in his rehabilitation cannot be overstated. One of the first people Beckham spoke to in the immediate aftermath of his sending off against Argentina was Fergie, who contacted him to offer some words of encouragement the following morning. He also made a point of telephoning Becks' parents.

He said he was 'sickened' by some of the flak directed against the player: 'There was a vindictiveness in many of the comments that made it obvious he was paying yet again for being more of a celebrity than any other footballer in Britain.' Referring to the support Beckham had been getting from Gary Neville, his closest football pal in the United and England squads, Fergie added: 'He can rely on a lot more help with getting over his depression when he reports at the club for the new season. That's the kind of club this is.'

Later, just before the start of the season, Fergie reiterated United's determination to help Beckham put his troubles behind him. Fergie said: 'I have already had my say on the viciousness of the reaction to his sending off and now I want to help him get back to normal. I have told him to forget all the daft talk about having to move abroad to escape the pressure, to keep his head down and enjoy his football with Manchester United.

'His parents have been staying with him and his father has been coming to training with him each day. They are giving him tremendous support. The lad has trained very well over the past week and, like the rest of us, he is eager to get our Championship challenge under way.'

Indeed, in United's first league match of the season at Leicester Beckham started as he meant to go on by scoring the goal – from a free-kick, naturally – which gave them a 2–2 draw. Far from unsettling him, the boos from opposition fans that marked his every touch of the ball seemed to drive him on.

That season he also scored against Everton, Aston Villa, Tottenham and Wimbledon (twice) in the Premiership, against Barcelona and Brondby in the European Champions League, and against Arsenal in the FA Cup semi-final. Needless to say, he also set up a number of goals for others.

United ended the season as the first team ever to win the Championship, European Champions League and FA Cup treble, and the first stage of Beckham's rehabilitation was complete. The second stage was provided by his success as England captain under Sven-Goran Eriksson.

During the qualifying competition for the 2002 World Cup in Korea and Japan, the change in the public perception of Beckham was provoked initially by his performances in two September 2001 matches. England's amazing 5–1 rout of Germany in Munich, one of the most notable in their history, and the 2–0 win over Albania at Newcastle's St James's Park lifted Eriksson's troops to the top of their group – some contrast to the forlorn-looking World Cup situation when he took over. Following those two matches, Beckham was widely singled out as having been one of England's most effective players.

After the Albania match, Eriksson rubber-stamped that impression enthusiastically: 'Beckham is a good footballer and a good captain. He is playing excellently, and he behaves like a captain. His first touch on the ball is excellent. In addition, he can run a lot and gets into good defensive positions. He is physically very strong and in this respect he gets better every time I see him.'

Eriksson, though, could hardly have anticipated the extent to which Beckham would emphasise all of these attributes the following month when England took on Greece at Old Trafford in their last qualifying match. For Beckham – not to mention SFX, the high-powered personal management company which has expertly cultivated his iconic status – the match was the ultimate image-enhancer. It seems difficult to believe that in the space of just over three years Beckham's fortunes could have been transformed so spectacularly.

In the pre-game build-up, Beckham talked about the way in which his role as England captain had helped change people's attitude to him. 'I drive through London and people give me the thumbs-up.' He made a joke of it by pausing as if in thought, and adding: 'No, they're definitely thumbs.' There can have been no doubt about that after the game.

Even before the kick-off Beckham carved a niche for himself in the hearts of 15 million televiewers as he walked on to the pitch holding the hand of 7-year-old Kirsty Howard, the little girl who has spearheaded a campaign to raise £5 million for a children's hospice and who was England's mascot for the game. Kirsty was born with her heart back to front, and has to have an oxygen cylinder with her all the time. It was trailing behind her as Beckham accompanied her gingerly on to the field, and the tenderness he displayed towards her was one of the most moving images of the football year.

The sight of Beckham looking as if he was playing Greece all on his own was equally memorable. England started the game with the belief that only a victory would see them pip Germany to an automatic place in the finals (a view based on the premise that Germany were bound to get maximum points from their match against Finland on the same day).

The home side were far below their best. When Greece went 1–0 and then 2–1 ahead, it was no more than they deserved. England were struggling; it seemed certain that they would have to endure the extra pressure of a play-off match if they were to qualify for the World Cup stage in Asia. But if there was any hope at all for England fans, it was in Beckham's ability to rise to the occasion in big matches.

The statistics of the performances of each England player in that game told their own story. In addition to the amount of ground Beckham covered, he was also well above the others in terms of his passing, tackling and interceptions. All his three free kicks were on target, putting him top of the list in the shots department as well. The third of those kicks, awarded for a foul on Teddy Sheringham around 30 yards from the Greek goal, came just 85 seconds from the end of the four minutes that the referee had – generously – added on as stoppage-time.

The Germany–Finland match had finished with the Germans held to a surprising 1–1 draw. So with England 'only' needing a draw, Beckham's run towards the ball was watched by millions holding their collective breath and praying. When Beckham found the top corner of the net with a curling kick shot remarkable even by his ultra-high standards, the sounds of cheering in emotion-charged households – and the packed Old Trafford stands – was something else.

Beckham's hero–zero–hero rehabilitation was complete, and it was maintained in the World Cup Finals, when England's 1–1 draw against Sweden was followed by Beckham steering them to their momentous 1–0 win over Argentina. It was typical of Beckham that, despite not being fully match fit, he should be the one to convert the 44th-minute penalty that gave England victory. The England full-back Danny Mills said: 'Full credit to Becks – he took an amazing penalty under enormous pressure. It takes a lot of heart to do that, a lot of bottle.' Not surprisingly, the theme was maintained by Eriksson: 'He is not 100 per cent fit yet. He has no problem with the foot [which he had broken before the World Cup Finals] but he needs games. To take a penalty in a match like this, when it's 0–0, showed that he is a good captain. Mentally, he is extremely strong.'

The memories of such Beckham moments have made it doubly difficult for his many admirers to come to terms with the decision by Ferguson and Manchester United to sell him to Real Madrid. Surely Fergie made a mistake – or did he?

Chapter Six

After the Divorce

Students of the supernatural must have had a field day with the rumour that the boot which struck Beckham belonged to Ole Gunnar Solksjaer. The Norwegian striker, whom Ferguson had been using mainly as a substitute, subsequently filled Beckham's role during the period when he was left out of the team. His surprisingly effective performances in a position that was comparatively alien to him clearly had a bearing on United's decision to sell Becks to Real Madrid.

Ferguson has always believed in having wide midfielders who can 'penetrate' defences, and Solksjaer can certainly do that. In August 2003, after Solksjaer had again looked good on the right side of midfield in United's matches in the United States, Fergie pointed out that the speed with which he had adjusted to the position was no more than he expected of a player with his 'football intelligence'. For his part, the 30-year-old Solksjaer modestly suggested that the change of roles had not been as radical for him as some might have thought. 'I have played there for Norway before, as well as on the left,' he explained. 'I have taken bits and pieces of my experience of playing in the position for Norway and brought them to my game at United.'

He pointed out that following Ruud Van Nistelrooy's arrival at Old Trafford, the terms of reference had changed for him and for the other potential Nistelrooy striking partners. 'Before Ruud's arrival, we played with two strikers,' he explained. 'But Ruud has become the top striker and his partner has played deeper or wider. So I have gradually got used to playing in a different way.'

Solksjaer's ability was not the only reason why Ferguson saw no need to be concerned about the absence of Beckham. Another was the potential of his new signings, notably midfielders Eric Djemba-Djemba and Kleberson – respectively Cameroon and Brazil internationals – and the ingenious 18-year-old Portuguese international forward Cristiano Ronaldo.

Bought from Sporting Lisbon for £12.24 million, a British record transfer fee for a teenager, Ronaldo did not waste time in showing what he could do for United. Brought on as a substitute in their opening Premiership match against Bolton when United were 1–0 ahead, his pace and dribbling skills did much to enable them to make it 4–0. It was hailed as the best United league debut by any player since George Best in the 1960s, and the headline above one newspaper report read 'Who needs Becks?'. It remains to be seen whether this will still be the message at the end of the season. But in view of the fans' reaction at the time of Beckham's transfer, few will be surprised if it is.

On the *Manchester Evening News* website Stuart Brennan wrote: 'Manchester United fans are split over the impending departure of David Beckham. Even hardcore Reds, who have despaired and sneered at the midfielder's increasingly ludicrous lifestyle, are arguing among themselves about the wisdom of flogging him – and especially flogging him to a major Champions League rival.

'But, after 13 years of unprecedented success, the bottom line is that those fans trust Fergie. If the manager sold Ruud Van Nistelrooy to Grimsby and brought in Vera Duckworth as his replacement, there are quite a few Reds who would back his judgement.'

Indeed, United fans have not had cause to bemoan the loss of any of the big-name players Fergie has sold in the past. The first sale that they initially found difficult to accept was the departure of England midfielder Paul Ince to Inter Milan in the summer of 1995. Ince, with his energy and fierce commitment, was a big Old Trafford crowd favourite. Someone had once described him as 'The Guv'nor', and he did, it is claimed, provoke some irritation by repeatedly drawing attention to the tag. Nevertheless, he commanded considerable dressing-room respect for his leadership qualities on the field.

When Fergie decided to part company with him, one Old Trafford insider confided that he thought the manager had taken leave of his senses. The Manchester United board were shocked, as were the fans. It even provoked the *Manchester Evening News* to run a poll on whether Fergie should be sacked – the result of which was in the affirmative.

Fergie's case was that Ince was getting too big for his boots. To Fergie, the most glaring example of this came in the 1995 FA Cup Final against Everton. Ince's main job was to sit in front of the United back-men in order to protect the defence. But he took it upon himself to surge forward with the ball, thus leaving a lot of space behind for Everton to exploit on the break. He took even more of a gamble when he tried to dribble around Everton defender Dave Watson. The ball was lost and Everton's counter-attack led to Paul Rideout scoring the only goal.

Fergie has said that Ince's attitude and performances 'had altered to a degree that I could not tolerate.' He added: 'I felt Paul was not playing to the discipline I demanded. He was not a bad person and had very generous traits, but if footballers think they are above the manager's control, there is only one word to be said to them – goodbye.'

It could easily have been goodbye to Fergie as well, if United had struggled without Ince. Instead, with Nicky Butt and Roy Keane more than matching Ince's tigerish midfield qualities, United achieved the Championship–FA Cup double the following season.

The controversial Keane, a player with arguably the most negative public image in the game, has become Ferguson's most coveted player at Old Trafford, although even Ferguson must have winced at some of the more extreme examples of Keane's combative personality –

notably the X-certificate tackle on Alf-Inge Haaland (which brought Keane one of his 11 red cards) and his astonishing bust-up with his Irish Republic manager Mick McCarthy (which led to Keane walking out on the Republic's 2002 World Cup squad). But despite all this, Ferguson admits that Keane – with his passion for the game and his hunger for success – reminds him of himself. Hence the fact that Fergie has publicly supported Keane through all of his hot-headed moments and made him United's captain. As long as Keane was at Old Trafford, there was no way that Beckham was going to get the honour.

Like Fergie, Keane is what the manager would readily describe as a 'real' football man. He is probably the last top-class footballer on Earth who could be expected to identify with the world that Beckham inhabits. He has made no secret of his distaste for what he has described as the 'phoneys, hangers-on and media whores' who surround footballers. There have been other verbal examples of his uncompromising attitude. Take his public rebuke of the strong corporate element in the Old Trafford crowd. Referring to the noise they made in support of the team (or rather the lack of it), Keane observed that they concentrated more on their 'prawn sandwiches' than on the football.

Keane felt it necessary to make a similar point about his team after United were knocked out of the European Champions League by Bayer Leverkuson at the semi-final stage in April 2002. In an emotional outburst – which some interpreted as a dig at Beckham in particular – Keane suggested that some United players had allowed the money they earned, and their lifestyles, to lead them away from the principles upon which their success had been based. He said: 'Rolex watches, garages full of cars, mansions, set up for life. Then they forgot about the game and lost the hunger that had got them the Rolexes, the cars and the mansions.' It could easily have been Fergie talking.

Such is Fergie's respect for Keane that many believe the player will end up taking over from him as United manager – a view strengthened by the fact that Keane has devoted some of his spare time to taking coaching courses. There has also been speculation that this was another reason why Beckham felt the time was right for him to move.

Referring to Ferguson's decision to retire and his subsequent U-turn, Paul Wilson pointed out in the *Observer*: 'Beckham would have been looking forward to a change at the top [and working under a manager who was more flexible and less tyrannical]. Instead, Beckham suddenly realised that there was to be no regime change, not now, not soon, not ever, in the context of his own playing career. Practically the first thing to happen after the managerial U-turn was Keane's signing up for another four years, becoming the club's best-paid player on £90,000 a week and pledging himself to United and Ferguson for the rest of his playing days. Keane's financial primacy did not last long once Beckham's image rights came into play [to give him financial parity with Keane] but for all the

England captain's enhanced world visibility, he became a more peripheral figure at Old Trafford from the day the Ferguson–Keane alliance was renewed.'

It is a reasonable assumption that Keane wasn't exactly gutted to see the back of Beckham, but he was philosophical about it when publicly giving his views on the transfer. He said: 'It is unfortunate because he is a top player, but the manager has sold a lot of top players over the years and the club have gone on. It does not matter who the player is. Players will always come and go. It is a business, and if the club get a good price for the player then they have to look at it. It is the same for everybody. It is the same for me. That's the way football is.'

Indeed, amid all the fuss about Beckham's move, this was something that tended to be overlooked. No player is expendable – they all have their price, and this has been shown in the transfers of a number of football figures more accomplished than Beckham.

Take some of the leading lights at Juventus. Since their brilliant coach Marcello Lippi joined the club in 1994, they have won the Italian Championship five times and lifted the European Champions League trophy. They have made four European Champions League Final appearances in all, the last in May 2003 when they lost to AC Milan on penalties. But throughout this period, Juventus – the biggest crowd-pullers in Italy but a club who needed transfer-market money to help fund their players' salaries – have repeatedly sold 'key' men. The list includes Gianluca Vialli, Fabrizio Ravanelli, Christian Vieri, Roberto Baggio and Zinedine Zidane.

All of them would have been happy to stay at Juventus, at least for a while. Zidane, the world's No. 1 player and the most expensive at the £48 million Real paid for him in July 2001, wanted to move to Spain partly because his wife is Spanish. But he was not bursting to get out of Juventus; he would have been willing to stay there for one more year. On his personal website

Zidane said: 'This transfer took place very rapidly, when in fact it was planned for next year. But in the end Juventus thought over Real's offer and finally decided that if a transfer was to happen, it should be this year. It was important for them to get a good deal of money out of the transfer deal.' This view was backed up by Juventus's general manager Luciano Moggi. He told the club's website: 'Zidane wanted a deal which would free him next year, on his terms and conditions [which would have meant Juventus getting only a third of the fee Real paid for him]. However, negotiations are conducted by the club, not by the players. We considered the fact that he wanted to go to Spain and we went ahead with it. To keep a player who has his mind set on going elsewhere is useless. Worse, it's damaging.'

Zidane helped Real win the European Champions League the following season. The difference that a footballing genius like him can make to a team was epitomised in the tightly contested final against Bayer Leverkuson, when he scored the goal which gave Real their 2–1 victory with a stunning volley. But Juventus have not done badly in the two seasons since his departure. They have twice won the Championship, after finishing runners-up in the two previous seasons; and in the 2002/03 season they beat Real Madrid in the semi-final of the European Champions League.

When it comes to getting their hands on any player they want, Real Madrid – thanks to their stature, charisma and willingness to spend money like water – are in a class of their own. Other cases have brought this into sharp focus: Luis Figo was bought by Real from Barcelona for £37.4 million in July 2000 and Ronaldo was secured from Inter Milan for £29.8 million in September 2002. Both players badly wanted to join Real, although in both instances the fans and the clubs they left behind were up in arms about their departure.

Figo was able to move because, under Spanish League transfer rules, any player has the right to change clubs by using the buy-out clause in his contract. Once Real Madrid had forked out his £37 million-plus buy-out fee, he was effectively out of contract.

In view of the fierce rivalry between Real and Barcelona, Figo's decision was courageous to say the least. In his first match at Barcelona as a Real player, which Barcelona won 2–0, missiles were thrown at Real's players every time they approached the touchline. Such was the bitterness directed at Figo that Real ordered him not to take any of their corners. The anti-Figo chants from the Barcelona fans referred to him as a 'whore' and the anti-Figo banners draped around the stadium displayed messages such as: 'You would sell your mother if you knew who she was.' Figo summed it up by saying that he felt as if he was 'in the skin of a murderer'. It is difficult to believe that Barcelona fans will ever totally forgive him for his move, which, of course, further underlines what a tremendous footballer he is.

Beckham fans have their own reason for looking upon Figo as an extra-special player following the recent revelation that when Figo was at Barcelona, Ferguson was interested in signing him for Manchester United, and wanted to offer Beckham in part-exchange. According to Michael Crick, the author of a book on Ferguson, the manager met Figo and his agent in a hotel near Lisbon in 2000, before the right winger – then the hottest football property in Europe – was due to play for his country against Denmark. Crick said: 'What made Ferguson's plans all the more audacious was that he wanted to swap Figo for David Beckham. It was the first sign that Ferguson was willing to part with the club's greatest star. It also showed his customary ruthlessness once he has decided a star player is no longer needed – acting without bothering to consult the player himself. On returning to Manchester, Ferguson got cold feet.'

Figo, who has operated mainly in the same position as Beckham, shows greater flair and ingenuity than him in open play. So, with Figo still going strong at Real, along with Zidane,

Ronaldo and Raul, the question of why the Spanish giants wanted Beckham is pertinent.

His commercial value to them – especially in their battle with United to dominate the mega-lucrative market in Asia – is one obvious explanation. Even the likes of Zidane, Ronaldo, Figo and Raul were taken aback by the public interest in Beckham on the club's four-match summer tour of Beijing, Tokyo, Hong Kong and Bangkok. It brought Real around £6 million and gave them the ideal launching pad to cash in on Beckham through television, merchandising and endorsements.

Brough Scott, covering Beckham's encouraging Real debut in Beijing for the *Sunday Telegraph*, noted that outside the Real team's hotel and on the approaches to the stadium visual signs of the popularity of other stars – on T-shirts and placards – were minuscule compared with those for Beckham. 'Then there was the screaming [during the game],' Scott added, pointing out that it was like being at a pop concert rather than a football match.

In Spain, too, Beckham is having a major financial impact, with clubs raising their admission prices considerably for Real matches.

In joining Real, Beckham has realised what millions would consider to be the ultimate fantasy. Manchester United are big, but if clubs are assessed on the number of major trophies they have won and their box-office appeal, Real are even bigger. Indeed, Beckham's place in that famous all-white strip is something that even Ferguson will envy about the player.

Like most others who saw it, Ferguson has never forgotten the game on which much of Real's charismatic appeal is based – the remarkable 7–3 win over Eintracht Frankfurt in the 1960 European Cup Final at Hampden Park. Fergie was then at the start of his career at Queen's Park, and as Hampden was the club's home he was able to watch the brilliant destruction of Eintracht from a good vantage point. Fergie thought he had seen it all when his beloved Rangers were outclassed by Eintracht in the semi-final – but the way they were mesmerised by Real was something else.

No team have dominated the European Cup (or European Champions League as it is now called) like Real Madrid. The win over Eintracht was their fifth successive triumph and their total of competition victories now stands at nine. They do like their silverwear in Madrid – the trophy room at Real's imposing Bernabeu Stadium is adorned by almost 1,500 trophies, and three women are employed there full-time to keep them clean.

However, the work they have to do is nothing compared with the sweat and toil to which many of Real's opponents are subjected in order to keep up with them. While Brazil have been the outstanding national team of modern times, Real have unquestionably been their closest equivalents in club football. They have repeatedly achieved a level of creativity in their play that is as close to Fantasy Football as any team could possibly get.

The move to Real, of course, has presented Beckham with a number of potential banana-skins – the language barrier, for example, and all the other problems associated with living and working in a foreign country. Moreover, in a Real dressing room also containing Zidane, Ronaldo, Figo and Raul, Beckham will surely find egos there bigger and more sensitive than those at Manchester United.

Raul, the captain and the most prolific goalscorer in Spanish football history, is acknowledged as the player with the biggest influence at Real. He and his supermodel wife Marmen Saz are Spain's Beck and Posh equivalents; and because of his playing record Raul is without doubt the most popular player among the fans. Suffice it to say that, in some of the decisions taken by Real's president and their coach, Raul was believed to have been the man in the background calling the shots. In making sure of Raul's support for him, it is just as well that Beckham is such a good crosser of the ball and sets up so many chances for strikers.

Recalling his playing experiences in Italy, David Platt, the England Under-21 coach, has said: 'Even the basic things [at Real] are going to be different. He will not be training just in the morning and then buzzing off by lunch-time to have a free afternoon shopping with Victoria. The big foreign clubs often do two [training] sessions a day, and you can eat with the team at the training ground as well.'

Steve McManaman, Beckham's only English teammate at Real, said: 'In England, new players are given a couple of seasons to fit in. Not here – it's sink or swim and most sink because you have to perform virtually from day one.' On the influence of Real club presidents, McManaman added: 'In England, politics [at boardroom level] never affects the players. Here, it is a fact of life the players have to deal with. You can be bought by one president of a club, who promotes you as his key asset, and the next year he can be gone.' Beckham hardly needed to hear that – Real's current president, Florentino Perez, the man who brought him to the club, is up for re-election in the summer of 2004.

The thought of how McManaman has fared in his four years at Real is not something that Beckham will want to dwell on either. The former Liverpool winger has had his good moments, such as scoring the second goal in Real's 3–0 European Champions League Final win over Valencia in 2000 and, even more notably for Real fans, the second goal in the 2–0 semi-final win at Barcelona in 2002 (Real's first victory there for 18 years). But McManaman has generally struggled to get into the starting line-up, and his England career has declined.

However, Beckham, while not possessing McManaman's ability to drift past players with the ball, is the more consistent and disciplined of the two. He is more of an all-round player, which is partly why he has come to Real at the right time.

To properly appreciate how he could prove an excellent buy for Real, it is necessary to look at the reasons why the club appointed Carlos Queiroz, Manchester United's assistant manager, as their new manager in the summer of 2003.

Queiroz was widely credited with having been mainly responsible for the defensive improvements at United that brought them the

Championship. There is also a need for him to improve this side of Real's game. Real have long been the most attack-conscious club team in the world. Their philosophy has been that, no matter how many goals the opposition might score as a result of their attacking boldness, Real will always score more. But this attitude can blow up in the team's faces occasionally and, while they are determined to remain true to their principles, Queiroz has been hired to bring more of a balance to their play.

He has already blown away the view that Beckham will suffer at Real because of the coach's admiration for Figo. Queiroz, as coach of the Portugal youth and senior teams, played a major part in Figo's development and the two men are known to be close friends. But when he joined Real, he immediately made it clear that Figo and Beckham should not be viewed as rivals for the right-side midfield spot; he was determined that both could be accommodated in the team, and he has shown this.

As for the ways in which Beckham can help improve Real, Queiroz has never been slow to recognise the England captain's work-rate and willingness to use his ability in the best interests of his teams. When the pair were at Manchester United, Beckham was one of the players Queiroz singled out as epitomising the importance of 'attitudes'. When he took over at Real Madrid, he said: 'Beckham will be very useful because he will bring the British footballing mentality and values like determination and bravery to the club.'

David Platt says that a player has to be exceptionally 'mentally strong' to play for a club like Real Madrid. Nobody can argue that Beckham lacks that toughness, so the next question is what this could lead to for him. The ultimate dream for Beckham fans (not to mention Beckham himself) is that he and Fergie will come face to face again in the new season's European Champions League Final, and that Becks – a Real hero already – will score in the last minute from one of those wonderful free kicks to give his team victory.

That really would be one in the eye for Fergie.

Bibliography

Best, George, and Collins, Roy, *Blessed – My Autobiography*, Random House, 2001

Cashmore, Ellis, *Beckham*, Blackwell, 2002

Crick, Michael, *Many Sides of Alex Ferguson*, Simon & Schuster, 2002

Ferguson, Alex, *Managing my Life*, Hodder & Stoughton, 1999

Fynn, Alex and Guest, Lynton, *For Love or Money*, Andre Deutsche, 1998

Gray, Eddie, *Marching on Together*, Hodder & Stoughton, 2001

Hansen, Alan, *A Matter of Opinion*, Partridge, 1999

Harrison, Eric, *The View from the Dugout*, The Parrs Wood Press, 2001

Hildred, Stafford and Ewbank, Tim, *There's Only One David Beckham*, David Blake, 2003

Hughes, Mark, *Hughesie! The Red Dragon*, Mainstream, 1994

Ridley, Ian, *Cantona, the Red and the Black*, Victor Gollancz, 1995

Tomas, Jason, *Soccer Czars*, Mainstream, 1996